THE
BLACK HAT
CHEF
COOKBOOK

THE
BLACK HAT CHEF COOKBOOK

by Chef René

A Lou Reda Book

HASTINGS HOUSE
MAMARONECK, N.Y.

Library of Congress Catalog Number: 87-062152

ISBN: 0-8038-9337-X

Second Printing

1 9 9 8 7 6 5 4 3 2

To my beloved wife, Ann, who (honestly) made me do this, and to my loving grandmother, who at age ninety-seven was still teaching me cooking tricks. She started my love for cooking when I was but six years old, and her Mohawk Indian teachings gave me the lust for life that I enjoy to this day.

ACKNOWLEDGMENTS

*H*undreds of people helped me get to where I am today. I want to thank so many, yet I get the feeling that I will miss some, so to them my sincere apologies.

First, I wish to honor the memory of my mentors from Les Chefs Internationale, The Black Hat Society: Joe Donon, Al Stockli, Patsy Mazzucelli, Papa Gino Leone, and Ted Baun.

Second, the old guard from the R.I. Professional Chefs Association: Gino Corelli, John Coressimo, Adolph Schrott, Charlie Arakalian, Bob Holland, Dick Roy, A. J. Morrone, and Dick Rampino.

To the new guard from the American Culinary Federation: Jeff Brooks, Michel Marcais, Paul Prudhomme, Emeril LaGasse, Mike Minor, Clarke Bernier, Robin Nixon, Mark Fitch, Joe Strangis, Stafford DeCambra, William Trask, Conrad Nonaka, Richard Reynolds, Wendell Rodrigues, Sam Choy, Maurice Fitzgerald, Carol Ann Reed, Debbie Kennedy, Susan Spicer, Leon Oppenheimer, Helmut Hamann, Al Constantine, Tom Bloodworth, Jason Kleinpeter, Jeff Smith, Phil Learned, Michel LeBorgne, George Karousos, Ted Butzbach, Bob Cribari, Johnny Rivers, Ruben Foster, Steve Pagano, Bert Cutino, Jack Braun, Fred Faria, John Bowen; the man who acts as our rep so well, Ed Brown; and, last but never least, for my respect for him is so great, chef Franz Lemoine. To these and to so many other members of this fantastic organization, for their continued contributions to the culinary field and for what they have come to mean to me, my most profound and humble thanks.

To those, also, from my new field, TV, who have also helped me: that fabulous Chinese chef-instructor, Martin Yan; the great Julia Child (and, no, it's not true, she never did drop a chicken on one of her shows); Roland, from Christian's in New Orleans, on the *Taste of New Orleans* shows; Jeff Smith, the Frugal Gourmet; and the one I have looked up to and whom I consider the best and a real friend, the former Galloping Gourmet, Graham Kerr—my sincerest thanks for all that you have taught me, given me, and done for me.

I want to give especial thanks to Sandy Richardson, my publisher, and Gilda Abramowitz, the editor of this book, for doing such a fantastic job, taking my jumbled array of mixed-up recipes and putting it together so beautifully.

Contents

Foreword

*W*ithout question, it was better to have met over a flat tire than a fallen soufflé.

I met Chef René (with black hat in place) over one such deflating experience (the tire, that is!). Our meeting was brief, but Richard is a colorful man, not easily forgotten. He is immediately personable.

His mark of friendship is his willingness to help. Richard is a natural born teacher. By carefully reading this book, you will learn the fine art of cooking from one of the most gifted and respected chefs.

Richard lives, cooks, and writes with intensity. His passion is absolute, his enthusiasm contagious. He really does want to be helpful. He has given his life in service, cooking for people who want good food. His techniques are professional and he communicates well.

Today, major changes are occurring in the style and manner of eating. Chef René gives you classic methods that stress essential flavor, and a presentation that lends itself equally to traditional dishes and the newer, lighter foods.

I'm truly honored to be his friend.

—*Graham Kerr,*
the former Galloping Gourmet

Introduction

A cookbook is nothing more than a guide to good eating—no more, no less. When it comes to cooking, the heart of the matter is not so much learning how to make certain dishes as how not to overseason, overcook, or overeat.

In using any cookbook, all you need to do is learn the ingredients, then approach the entire thing with a feeling of having made up the recipe yourself. Gain as much confidence as you possibly can, and remember, from the first, that you are the chef and the dish is to please you, not your guest or guests. After all, most of the time you are cooking to feed yourself and your family. Your taste is what really counts, so feel free to adjust the types and amounts of ingredients called for in a recipe. Make it yours.

Follow your instincts, make it taste the way you like, serve only the amount you feel is right, and you will seldom make mistakes.

From the Chef's Notebook

To core an apple that will be cooked whole, use a tool made just for that purpose—but if the apple is to be cut up, quarter it, then slice out the core with a paring knife.

If a stubborn jar top refuses to yield, turn the jar upside down, tap the cover around its edges, then just twist and off it comes.

Never use a damp towel or potholder to take a hot pot off the heat or out of the oven. Heat turns the moisture to scalding steam.

To get the maximum volume from eggs for soufflés or omelettes, separate them when they are cold and let them come to room temperature before whipping them up.

Lemons have innumerable uses. They are the finest of tenderizers for meats (papaya juice works well, too), and fish should never be served without them.

Got the smell of garlic or onions on your hands? Rub a cut lemon on them.

Want cut-up fresh fruit to keep its color? Soak it in water with some lemon juice in it. Add a dash of lemon juice (or vinegar) to the water when cooking beets or red cabbage; this helps keep it red.

If long-refrigerated lemons have dried out, simmer them in boiling water for a few minutes, then pierce one end and squeeze. You will be surprised at how much juice comes out.

The greatest marinade for meat is 1/4 cup lemon juice, 1/2 cup olive oil, 2 crushed garlic cloves, 1 finely chopped small onion, oregano, salt, and crushed pepper. To tenderize a cheap cut of meat, marinate it in papaya juice.

If you need softened butter, but forgot to take it out of the refrigerator or freezer, simply grate it. To serve butter decoratively for a special guest, whip it with a little cream and squeeze it out of a pastry tube with a star tip.

If cheese seems always to stick to the grater, rub oil on the grater first.

If you are planning to serve a soufflé but will be pressed for time, prepare it up to the point of adding the egg whites. At serving time, beat the egg whites, fold them in, and bake.

If you have trouble with soggy pie crusts, brush them with egg white and dust with flour. If it's only the bottom that gives you trouble, just dust it with flour and sugar.

If your soup is too salty, a peeled and quartered raw potato will absorb much of the excess.

There are many ways to rescue a curdled hollandaise. Take the pan off the heat and whisk in hot water, a spoonful at a time, until it regains its smoothness. Or take it off the heat, throw in a small handful of chipped ice, and whisk vigorously until smooth. Or take it off the heat and whisk in chilled cream. If none of these works, put it in a blender and homogenize it. This works every time.

If you are going to broil a great deal of food at once, put a few slices of dry bread under the rack. They will absorb most of the fat drippings and prevent smoking and possibly a fire.

To freshen the flavor of frozen vegetables, add a pinch of sugar to the cooking water.

If a sauce is somewhat lumpy or not as smooth as you would like, just strain it. If you want to thicken it, purée the solids and whisk in.

Most sauces should never be cooked above a simmer, especially butter sauces (which often are made with delicate egg yolks, too).

To make a gravy or sauce to accompany a pan-fried dish, pour a little champagne or club soda into the pan and scrape up the browned particles stuck to the bottom.

Do you often cook wild game? Use vinegar in the marinade or even just to wash off the game. It reduces the wild taste.

If your rice comes out sticky, try browning it first in oil or butter. This gives it a nutty flavor, too. To reheat rice, put it in a sieve over a pan of simmering water, cover it, and steam it for about 5 minutes.

Raisins and other fruit tend to sink to the bottom of cake batters. To prevent this, flour them before adding them to the batter.

Have trouble applying frosting to a cake? Dust the cake with a bit of flour or cornstarch first. If cake icings always seem to become grainy, add a pinch of salt. To keep icing moist, add a bit of baking powder to the confectioner's sugar.

A bouquet garni consists of herbs (1 marjoram sprig, 2 parsley sprigs, 2 thyme sprigs, 1 small bay leaf) wrapped in a piece of cheesecloth; it is dropped into the pot, then removed and thrown away when the cooking is done. Instead of cheesecloth, you can put the herbs in an aluminum tea ball—cheap and reusable.

Chocolate can be tricky to work with. The next time you have to melt some, grease the pan first. The chocolate will pour out more easily and less of it will stick to the pan.

For an easy dessert, dip the ends of strawberries, grapes, or other fruit in melted chocolate, chill on a rack in the refrigerator, and serve with cheeses and/or champagne or wine.

If you are like me, you always have trouble with the membrane of an orange—you know, the white part that sticks to the part you want to eat. To get around that, soak the orange in hot water for about 5 minutes, then peel it. Refrigerate it to the desired serving temperature.

Uh-oh—you whipped heavy cream too much and it turned to butter. To rescue it, add a bit of milk and beat it in very carefully. It will turn back into whipped cream.

Speaking of whipping, you can whisk for a long time without getting tired if you alter your grip. Use a thick-handled whisk; instead of grasping it from above, hold it against your palm, between the thumb and forefinger, with the thumb standing up and the forefinger bent down. Use the other three fingers to snap the whisk handle repeatedly against your palm.

Sometimes you reach for an ingredient only to find that you are out of it. These substitutes can be used without altering the flavor of the dish: To replace 1 cup buttermilk, add 1 tablespoon vinegar or lemon juice to 1 cup milk and let stand for 5 minutes. Instead of sour cream, add a bit of vinegar or lemon juice to sweet cream and let stand for an hour (or use plain yogurt). For corn syrup, substitute sugar plus more of the liquid called for in the recipe. You can use undiluted evaporated milk instead of light cream. To replace 1 tablespoon baking powder, use 1 teaspoon baking soda plus 2 teaspoons cream of tartar. To replace 1 tablespoon flour for thickening, use 1/2 tablespoon cornstarch or 2 teaspoons quick-cooking tapioca.

Do not salt vegetables too soon before serving or they will lose most of their vitamins. Salt them just before serving (if you must use salt at all). For the same reason, cut them up just before you cook them.

Cooking garlic excessively makes it bitter. Just brown it—the lighter the color, the sweeter the flavor.

You can preserve certain seasonings in oil or vinegar. I like fresh dill very much, but cannot carry the plants when I travel, so I soak some in light oil and use it when I want the flavor to be real. Remember that preserved and frozen seasonings are more concentrated than fresh, so use less of them.

Hard-boiled (actually, long-simmered) eggs are a problem for many. To prevent cracking, take them out of the refrigerator half an hour ahead of time and stick a pin in the rounded end. Another way is to add salt, lemon juice, or vinegar to the water; this will keep the egg from coming out even if the shell does crack. If you have trouble peeling them, cook the eggs for 3 to 5 minutes, crack the shells all around with a knife handle, and cook for another 10 minutes. Take them out of the water and run cold water on them as you peel them.

Learn to know your oven's hot spots and cold spots. Take five slices of bread and place them on the middle rack, in all four corners and one in the center. Set the temperature at 400° and toast the slices, checking every so often to see which one becomes brown first and which reaches that stage last.

Saffron is one of the most expensive seasonings you could ever have occasion to buy. Would you believe it costs more than $2,000 a pound ($2,064)? If you want to make a dish that calls for it, buy a small container (0.007 ounce). The recipe will usually call for water, such as: "Cook the rice in 3 cups water flavored with saffron." Okay—add chicken base* to the water and *one eighth* the amount of saffron called for. You will be surprised—as I was—to find that the flavor actually carries

* From L. J. Minor Corp.—see page 31.

through the dish just as though you had put in the whole amount of saffron.

Here is a remarkable trick that works like a charm. You could cook vegetables in water, then sauté them in butter or oil and add seasonings— or simply put water in the bottom of a steamer, along with white wine, lemon juice, pepper, and the seasonings you want to incorporate into the vegetable. Let's assume that you are cooking carrots and cauliflower. Cut up the carrots and add fresh dill to the liquid in the steamer. When the carrots are almost done, add the cauliflower florets and finish them off. You can season any vegetable with any flavor just by adding the seasonings and herbs to the steaming water.

Keep in Mind...

*T*hroughout the recipes, unless otherwise indicated:

"Butter" means unsalted butter.

"Pepper" means fresh ground black pepper; use white pepper for light-colored sauces and dishes.

"Flour" means all-purpose unbleached white flour. For baking, sift it before measuring, then sift it together with the other dry ingredients to disperse them evenly.

Potatoes, apples, etc., need not be peeled unless you like to peel them.

Generally, 1 tablespoon fresh herb equals 1 teaspoon dried herb.

Use pasteurized heavy cream, not ultrapasteurized, which has a cooked flavor and does not whip successfully.

Eggs are large.

Recommended seasonings such as Paul Prudhomme's Seafood Magic Seasoning, Creole mustard, and hoisin sauce are available in "gourmet" or ethnic food sections of many supermarkets. If you use prepared horseradish, read the label and buy a brand free from preservatives and other chemicals.

To grease a pan for baking, use butter or margarine, not oil.

Always preheat the oven to the desired temperature; many dishes need that initial blast of hot air to come out properly.

To make a roux, melt butter and in it cook an equal amount of flour over low heat for 4 to 6 minutes.

To prepare a mirepoix, cut celery, carrots, and onions into 1/2-inch dice.

Canned tomatoes come in a bewildering variety of sizes. Buy the size closest to what is called for in a recipe.

Feel free to multiply or divide recipes according to how many you have to feed.

APPETIZERS AND FIRST COURSES

*M*any of us wish to make an impression on guests whom we invite home for a classical dinner, so we try to serve something completely different and out of the ordinary. Hors d'oeuvres and canapés do that for us, but many are too well known. Here are a few that you can do quite easily, yet are different and impressive. Plan to serve more per person as a first course than as an appetizer.

STUFFED CHERRY TOMATOES

24	cherry tomatoes	3	tablespoons minced celery
1¹/2	tablespoons minced shallots	8	ounces cream cheese
3	tablespoons sour cream	1	tablespoon French brandy
4	tablespoons chopped pecans		White pepper
		24	parsley sprigs

*D*ig out the inside of each tomato to make a well for the filling. Mix all of the other ingredients, except the parsley, and fill the tomatoes with the mixture. Chill them for as long as you wish. When ready to serve, place a small sprig of parsley in the center of the filling and put the tomatoes on a serving platter.
Serves 10 to 12

EGGVIAR

4 eggs
1 jar black caviar (beluga)

*P*urchase a syringe that has a needle at least 1/8 inch in diameter. With an electric drill, drill a hole just a bit larger than the syringe tip size in the top of each raw egg. Insert the syringe into the egg; withdraw part of the albumen and discard it. Fill the syringe with caviar and insert it into the egg. Tape the hole with waterproof tape, then boil the eggs for at least 8 minutes, run cold water on them, and peel them right away. Slice the eggs and serve the slices on rounds of toast or Melba toast rounds.
Serves 8

This one will flip their wig. It is difficult, I know, but so well worth the effort that you will be envied for your talent.

STUFFED EGGS

8   eggs
2   large tablespoons
      prepared horseradish
4   ounces ham
3   tablespoons mayonnaise

2   tablespoons semisweet
      white wine
Salt
White pepper

*H*ard-boil the eggs and chill them. Cut them in half length-wise. Remove the yolk and mix it with the other ingredients. Using a pastry tube with a star tip, fill the egg cavities. You can sprinkle on paprika or finely chopped parsley, if you like.
   Serves 8

RAW VEGETABLE DIP

1/2   pint heavy cream,
        whipped
4   ounces cream cheese
2   tablespoons French
        brandy
1   garlic clove, finely
        minced

6   tablespoons finely
        chopped fresh
        parsley
1/4   cup sour cream
4   ounces plain yogurt
1   small onion, minced
      White pepper

*B*lend all of the ingredients in a food processor. Chill well and serve on a platter, surrounded by raw cauliflower, broccoli, celery sticks, carrot sticks, and so on.
   Serves 10 to 12

People have come to realize that raw vegetables, served properly, are better for them than cooked. Try this dip to add variety.

CURRIED KING CRAB MEAT

8 ounces cream cheese
1 garlic clove, minced
1 tablespoon *hot* curry
   powder
  Salt
  Pepper
2 tablespoons heavy
   cream

2 teaspoons minced
   onion
2 tablespoons chopped
   fresh parsley
12 ounces crab meat,
   chopped into small
   pieces

*M*ix all of the ingredients until quite well blended. Spread the mixture on pieces of bread cut to any shape you like—stars, rounds, rectangles, or the like. Bake in the oven at 325° for about 15 minutes. Serve hot or cold.
Serves 10 to 12

PUFF PASTRY TARTILLANS

1 8-ounce package frozen
   spinach
1 tablespoon minced
   onion
4 hard-boiled eggs

4 tablespoons grated
   cheddar cheese
24 4-inch squares of puff
   pastry (page 183)
  Melted butter

*P*urée the spinach, onion, eggs, and cheese. Set aside. Brush the pastry squares on the bottom with melted butter, place them on a cookie sheet, and brush the tops with water. Place a spoonful of the filling in the center of each square. Pull the opposite corners together, and try to pinch the four corners together to form a bundle. Bake in a preheated 400° oven until you see the pastry turn a rich golden brown. Serve hot or cold, as you prefer.
Serves 10 to 12

CHEESY CANAPÉS

96	slices cheese (any kind)	12	slices black olives
96	toasted bread pieces	12	small cooked shrimp,
1	small jar red caviar		peeled and deveined
1	small jar black caviar	4	large radishes, sliced
12	slices pepperoni	4	small slices of a good
4	hard-boiled eggs,		ham
	grated	12	slices chicken
12	slices green olives		

*P*lace the cheese on the bread. Heat them in a 400° oven, 12 at a time, to soften and melt the cheese. Then top each piece with any combination of the toppings in the ingredients. For example, place a shrimp and a sprinkling of grated egg on one. On another place a slice of ham, to fit the shape of the canapé, and on it a slice of olive. For still another, use a piece of chicken with a slice of radish. It is that easy; just use your imagination.
Makes 96

Canapés are an appetizer that can be served with delight if you do something different with them.

First, you should know what to serve them on and how to prepare what you will be using. Bread should almost always be used; get a firm type that will stand up to toasting or frying. A good bakery can provide it for you. Just tell them what you intend, and they can sell you the right product.

Second, purchase a set of cookie cutters in different shapes. Use these to cut out the canapé bases. Butter the cut bread-figures and bake them in a 360° oven for 15 minutes or more. When they turn brown, take them out and remove them from the pan right away. You could fry them in a skillet if you wished, but the oven method is better.

OYSTER CANAPÉS

18	shucked oysters, with their liquor		Butter
1/4	cup hollandaise sauce (page 245)	12	1½-inch bread rounds
		2	tablespoons minced fresh parsley

Put the oysters and their liquor in a skillet or saucepan and cook over low heat just until they seem plump and the edges ruffle up. Drain the oysters and chop them. Combine with the hollandaise sauce. Butter the bread rounds on one side and sauté them in a pan until they are just browned on that side only. Mound the oyster mixture on the uncooked side and sprinkle with parsley. Gently press the parsley into the oyster mixture so that it adheres. Dot each canapé with a dab of butter. Place on a baking sheet and heat through in a preheated 375° oven. Serve 3 per person.

Serves 4

THE BATTER OF BATTERS—WITH BEER

2	cups flour	2	tablespoons baking powder
	Large pinch of salt	1	can or more flat beer

Mix the flour, salt, and baking powder; then mix the beer in slowly until the batter becomes semithick. Dip what you wish to serve—shrimp, oysters, clams, fish, or the like—in the batter. Cook in deep fat heated to 400° to 425°.

Serves 12

A very old and dear friend and mentor, chef Albert Stockli, from the Stonehenge Inn in Connecticut, taught me this beer batter for canapés, one of the best I have ever tried.

OYSTERS MOSCA

Italian bread crumbs
Olive oil
1   quart shucked oysters,
      with their liquor
Fresh garlic juice (from
      a press)
Rosemary

Minced garlic
Oregano
Crushed whole
      peppercorns
Chopped or ground
      bacon

*P*lace a coating of bread crumbs on the bottom of a baking pan large enough to hold the oysters, and moisten it with olive oil. Lay the oysters on top and add their liquor, along with the seasonings. Place another coating of bread crumbs over the entire pan and sprinkle with oil. Then place a modest portion of bacon on top. Bake at 400° until golden brown.

Serves 24

Mr. Mosca taught me this himself, at L'Enfant's Restaurant in New Orleans.

OYSTERS BIENVILLE

4   tablespoons butter
8   shallots
2   tablespoons flour
1   cup chicken stock
1   cup chopped cooked
      small shrimp
8   ounces mushrooms,
      finely chopped
2   egg yolks
1/2   cup dry white wine

12   oysters, opened and
        left in the bottom
        shell
1/2   cup bread crumbs
2   tablespoons grated
        Parmesan cheese
Paprika
Salt
Pepper

*M*elt the butter in a large saucepan. Finely chop the shallots and sauté them in the butter. Add the flour and make a roux by cooking it for about 5 minutes over a low flame. Add the chicken stock, shrimp, and mushrooms. Cook briefly. Beat together the egg yolks and wine and add to the saucepan. Cook until slightly thickened. Top each oyster with the mixture. Combine the bread crumbs, Parmesan, and a little paprika, salt, and pepper, and sprinkle over the sauce. Bake in a preheated 375° oven until it shows a slight browning on top. Serve 3 per person, with a slice of lemon on the side.

Serves 8

OYSTERS ROCKEFELLER

1/3	cup butter	1/2	teaspoon salt
11/4	cups frozen chopped spinach, thawed	1/2	teaspoon white pepper
	Large pinch of nutmeg	3/4	cup bread crumbs
		1	jigger Pernod
3 to 4	tablespoons minced onion	12	oysters, opened and left in the bottom shell

*M*elt the butter in a large saucepan and add all of the remaining ingredients, except the oysters. Cook briefly and place on top of the oysters in the bottom shell. Bake in a preheated 375° oven until somewhat dry on top. Serve 3 per person, with a lemon wedge on the side.

Serves 6

BAKED OYSTERS WITH FINES HERBES

11/2	sticks (3/4 cup) butter	2	teaspoons lemon juice
9	shallots, grated		Salt
1/4	cup minced fresh parsley		Pepper
1/4	cup minced chives	36	oysters on the half shell
1/4	cup cracker crumbs		

*M*ake a paste with all of the ingredients, except the oysters. Line a small baking sheet pan with rock salt. Cover the oysters with the paste and set on the rock salt. Bake in a preheated 400°

oven for approximately 10 minutes, until the oysters are plump.

Serves 6

A favorite from the collection of my Associate Chef Danny McDole, on my TV series.

STUFFED CLAMS OR OYSTERS

18	cherrystone clams or oysters	2	tablespoons dry white wine
4	tablespoons lemon juice	1/2	tablespoon crushed red pepper
2	cups bread crumbs or cracker crumbs		Just a bit of salt

*R*emove the clams or oysters from their shells. Chop them into small pieces. Mix the lemon juice, bread crumbs, wine, pepper, and salt. Add the chopped clams or oysters. Fill the shells with this mixture and bake at 400° until the top becomes crusty. Serve 3 per person, with a lemon wedge on the side.

Serves 6

CRAB MEAT SHIMODA

1	celery stalk	2	large pinches of minced fresh dill
1	onion, minced		
1/2	pint heavy cream		Several pinches of Paul Prudhomme's Seafood Magic Seasoning
1/2	pint sour cream		
1/2	pint plain yogurt		
1/4	cup mayonnaise		
7 to 8	tablespoons dry white wine		
2	tablespoons lemon juice	12 to 18	ounces crab meat Lettuce leaves

*V*ery finely grind the celery and onion in a food processor or a blender. Whip the cream until thick. Add the sour cream and whip again. Add the yogurt and mayonnaise and whip again. Mix in the celery, onion, wine, lemon juice, dill, and seafood seasoning. Put a lettuce leaf on each appetizer dish. Place a generous amount of the sauce on it, and 2 to 3 ounces of crab meat.

Serves 6

I developed this dish for the Delta Point River Restaurant in Vicksburg, Mississippi. The Automobile Association of America awarded the restaurant four stars a mere thirteen days after it opened.

CRAB MEAT STUFFING FOR MUSHROOMS, SHRIMP, OR FISH

12	large club crackers	4	tablespoons chopped fresh parsley
8	tablespoons melted butter (1 stick)	4	tablespoons sauterne
1/4	tablespoon crushed red pepper		
	Juice of 1/2 lemon	12	large mushrooms, or
4	ounces king crab meat, chopped		12 large shrimp, or 6 flounder or sole fillets

*C*rush the crackers to a semifine grind. Add the next six ingredients and mix to a soft, pasty consistency.

To stuff mushrooms, remove the stems, mound the stuffing in the caps, place in a buttered pie tin, and bake in a preheated 400° oven for 12 to 15 minutes. For shrimp, peel them, leaving on the tails, devein them, and stuff; bake in a buttered pie tin in a preheated 400° oven for 12 to 15 minutes. For fish, spread the stuffing on the skin side of the fillets and roll up. Place them on a buttered pie tin, rub them with butter and lemon juice, and bake in a preheated 375° oven for 20 minutes.

Serves 4 to 6

SNAILS IN MUSHROOMS

16 small mushroom caps
2 sticks (1 cup) butter
6 tablespoons finely
   minced garlic

4 tablespoons chopped
   fresh parsley
2 tablespoons dry white
   wine
16 snails

*C*lean the mushroom caps and set them in a baking dish. Soften the butter and mix it with the garlic, parsley, and wine. Place some of the mixture in the mushroom caps, top each with a snail, and generously cover the snail with more of the mixture. Bake at 400° until the mushrooms are cooked, 4 to 6 minutes or even more, if needed, until the mixture is completely melted. Serve 4 per person.

Serves 4

SHRIMP COCKTAIL

1/2 bottle ketchup
2 tablespoons lemon
   juice
5 to 6 tablespoons hot
   prepared
   horseradish

4 large lettuce leaves
16 medium-size
   shrimp, peeled,
   deveined, and
   cooked

*M*ix the ketchup, lemon juice, and horseradish. Make it as hot as you like. Place a lettuce leaf, whole or chopped into small pieces, in each serving dish and top it with sauce. Arrange 4 shrimp either on the lettuce or around the edge of it.

Serves 4

Most people have the impression that a good shrimp cocktail sauce has to have Worcestershire sauce, Tabasco sauce, onion, and chili sauce in it to make it right. Wrong. Try this one. You will be surprised at how easy it is—and economical.

SHRIMP RÉMOULADE

16 medium-size shrimp, peeled and deveined
2 tablespoons olive oil
1 tablespoon cider vinegar
1/2 teaspoon paprika
White pepper
1 tablespoon prepared hot mustard (Creole type, if possible)
1/2 teaspoon drained prepared horseradish
1/2 celery stalk, very finely chopped
1 teaspoon grated onion
1 teaspoon minced fresh parsley
Salt
Salad greens

*P*ut the shrimp in a pot of cold water with a bit of salt added. Bring to a boil, then turn off the heat and let the shrimp sit in the water for a few minutes. Drain and let cool. Combine all of the remaining ingredients, except the salt and greens. Season the sauce with salt, a bit at a time. Refrigerate the sauce for at least an hour. Make a bed of crisp greens on each serving plate. Put 4 shrimp on each and cover with sauce.
Serves 4

SHRIMP AND CUCUMBER SALAD

Vinegar Dressing

4 tablespoons rice wine vinegar
1/2 teaspoon salt
4 teaspoons sugar
2 teaspoons dark soy sauce

16 shrimp, peeled and deveined
2 small cucumbers
1 teaspoon salt
2 tablespoons sesame seeds

*M*ix the dressing ingredients and shake well to blend. Cook the shrimp, cut into bite-size pieces, and chill well. Peel and seed the cucumbers and cut them into very thin slices. Sprinkle them with salt and marinate for at least an hour. Mix the shrimp and cucumbers and toss with the dressing. Sprinkle with sesame seeds and serve in small appetizer dishes.

Serves 4

Note: Some prefer to roast the sesame seeds. I do not, but the choice is yours.

SQUID IN TOMATO SAUCE

1	pound squid	1/2	cup dry sherry
4	tablespoons olive oil	1	cup solid-pack
2	garlic cloves		tomatoes
	Salt	1	teaspoon chopped
	Pepper		fresh parsley
	Large pinch of		
	oregano		

*C*lean the squid and cut into small ringlike pieces. Heat the olive oil in a saucepan and brown the garlic in it for about 2 to 3 minutes; do not let it burn. Add the squid, cover, and cook for 10 minutes. Turn the heat off for a few minutes, then turn it on again and add the salt, pepper, oregano, and sherry. Cook for another 10 minutes. Turn the heat off again for a few minutes. Turn the heat back on, add the tomatoes and parsley, and cook for another 15 minutes. Serve very hot, on toast.

Serves 4

Note: Squid is very chewy—it can even be called tough. However, turning the heat off between each cooking step lets it marinate in its juices, tenderizing it. Do all the cooking over low heat.

FRIED SQUID

1 1/2	pounds very small squid	1/2	cup dry white wine
1/2	cup olive oil	1/2	teaspoon salt
1	large garlic clove	1/8	teaspoon dried
1	cup tomato sauce		ground red pepper

*C*lean the squid and wash it thoroughly. Heat the oil in a preheated saucepan. Brown the garlic and discard it. Cook the squid over low to medium heat for 10 minutes. Turn the heat off for a few minutes. Add the tomato sauce, wine, salt, and pepper. Cover and cook for 15 minutes. Serve with a loaf of French or Italian bread on the side.

Serves 4

MARINATED CRAB CLAWS

16	crab claws	2	tablespoons lemon juice
1/4	cup red wine vinegar		
1/2	teaspoon tarragon leaves	5	garlic cloves, finely minced
1/2	cup minced green pepper	1/2	cup finely chopped fresh parsley
1/2	cup minced celery	1/4	teaspoon salt
1/2	cup minced scallions	1/4	teaspoon sugar
1/2	teaspoon black pepper	4	tablespoons dry vermouth
1/2	cup olive oil		

*I*f the crab claws are purchased already cooked, just crack them, remove half of the shells, and set the claws in the refrigerator. If they are raw, steam them lightly and set aside to cool. Mix all of the remaining ingredients and refrigerate. When ready to serve, place the claws in a large serving bowl and cover with the marinade. Use a slotted spoon to pick up the claws. Serve with small French bread rolls on the side.

Serves 4

CRAWFISH ÉTOUFFÉE

2	sticks (1 cup) butter	1/4	cup chopped green pepper
1/2	cup flour		
2	cups chopped onions	1/2	tablespoon minced garlic
1/4	cup chopped celery		

16	crawfish tails	1/4	cup chopped scallions,
1/2	teaspoon salt		white part only, or
1	teaspoon black pepper		1/4 cup chopped
1/2	teaspoon cayenne		shallots
	pepper	1/2	tablespoon lemon juice
1/8	teaspoon crushed red	1/2	tablespoon minced
	pepper		fresh parsley
1	large pinch of cumin	1/2	cup cold water

*I*n a heavy 4- to 5-quart kettle over low heat, melt the butter. Gradually add the flour, and cook over low heat until it reaches a medium brown color. Cook slowly and stir almost continuously, to avoid burning. Add the onions, celery, green pepper, and garlic and cook, stirring often, until the vegetables are done, 15 to 20 minutes. Add the crawfish tails, salt, black pepper, cayenne, red pepper, cumin, scallions, lemon juice, and parsley. Add the cold water and bring to a boil; then lower the heat and simmer for 25 to 30 minutes.

Serves 6

Really Cajun! This dish can be served in many ways. Cajuns love it on rice. I like to serve it on squares of puff pastry or several layers of Greek phyllo pastry. I cut 4-inch squares of phyllo, butter them, and bake at 400° for about 12 minutes. Once it has reached a nice golden brown, it is done. Just spoon 4 of the crawfish tails with some of the sauce onto rice or pastry—and enjoy!

STUFFED BONELESS CHICKEN WINGS

12	middle sections of	2	tablespoons hoisin
	chicken wings		sauce
12	strips green peppers	4	tablespoons sake
12	slices Chinese	1/2	cup coconut milk
	mushrooms	1	tablespoon lemon juice
12	slices water chestnuts		

*C*ut the end of the bone from the middle section of each chicken wing. Push out the bone and stuff one piece of pepper, mushroom, and water chestnut into the cavity. Make a marinade of the hoisin sauce, sake, coconut milk, and lemon juice. Soak the chicken pieces in this for 30 to 60 minutes, then cook them in it. Serve 3 per person.

Serves 4

POP-A-CORNY CHICKEN

Mild cheese
Leftover cooked chicken
Popped popcorn, ground up

*M*elt the cheese over low heat. Cut the chicken into pieces, dip them in the cheese, and roll in the popcorn. Serve on long toothpicks.

Note: In a pinch, you could use Cheez Whiz and Cheez Doodles.

Short of putting a piece of cheese on a cracker, they don't come much easier than this. It's good, too.

CUBED CHICKEN WRAPPED IN SMOKED SALMON OR PROSCIUTTO

Marinade

2	tablespoons hoisin sauce	2	tablespoons dark soy sauce
1	cup sake	1/2	onion, grated
1	tablespoon grated ginger root	4	tablespoons oyster sauce
4	tablespoons light brown sugar		
2	chicken breasts, boned and cut into 1-inch cubes	1	piece smoked salmon or prosciutto per cube of chicken
6	tablespoons sesame oil		

*C*ombine the marinade ingredients. Marinate the chicken for 4 hours. Heat the sesame oil in a pan and sauté the chicken until just done. Wrap each cube with salmon or prosciutto and secure with a toothpick.

Serves 4

CHICKEN LIVER PÂTÉ

1 small onion, chopped	16 tablespoons sauterne
4 tablespoons butter	16 slices bacon, cooked
16 chicken livers	and crumbled
Juices of 2 lemons	4 hard-boiled eggs

*S*auté the onion in butter until translucent. Add the livers and cook for 4 to 5 minutes. Add the lemon juice and wine. Reduce the heat and cook until dry. Put the livers, bacon, and eggs in a food processor or blender and mix until smooth. Mound the mixture on a plate and chill before serving.

Serves 4

RUMAKI, JAPANESE STYLE

16 chicken livers	4 tablespoons oyster
16 bamboo shoots or	sauce
water chestnuts	4 tablespoons sake
8 slices bacon, blanched	1/2 tablespoon dark soy
and cut in half	sauce
2 tablespoons hoisin	2 tablespoons dark
sauce	brown sugar

*W*rap a slice of chicken liver (or a whole liver, if you prefer) and a piece of bamboo shoot or water chestnut in a half slice of bacon. Marinate in a mixture of hoisin sauce, oyster sauce, sake, and soy sauce, and sugar. Bake in a preheated 350° oven until the bacon becomes slightly crisp. Turn once. Use the marinade to keep them slightly moist when baking. Make a duk sauce out of the rest of the marinade with the addition of a little oyster sauce.

Serves 4

SWISS FONDUE

1 pound Swiss cheese	1/2 cup semidry white wine
2 tablespoons arrowroot powder	1 teaspoon lemon juice
Butter	1/16 teaspoon grated nutmeg
2 garlic cloves, minced	White pepper
1 1/2 cups dry white wine	1/4 cup kirsch

*C*hop the cheese into small pieces; sprinkle the arrowroot over it and let it sit. Put the fondue pot over low heat. Melt a bit of butter in it and sauté the garlic. Take out the garlic and throw it away. Put the wines in the pot and heat slightly. Add the lemon juice. Using a wooden spoon, stir in the cheese, a bit at a time, melting each amount before adding more. Turn the heat up just a bit; as soon as the cheese is all melted and begins to bubble, add the nutmeg and pepper, then the kirsch. Serve it in the pot with fondue forks, and use chunks of French or Italian bread for dipping.

Serves 12 or more

Variations: Hot Pepper Fondue. Substitute a pound of hot pepper cheese for the Swiss cheese.

Cheesy Double Fondue. Use 1/2 pound each Gruyère and caraway cheese instead of the Swiss cheese.

PEAR WRAPPED IN HOT ITALIAN HAM

2 ripe pears
8 slices prosciutto or
  other spicy Italian
  ham

1 large container pear-
  flavored yogurt

*P*eel the pears. Core them and cut into quarters. Wrap each quarter with a slice of ham. Spread a layer of the yogurt on the bottom of each serving plate and place a pear quarter on top. Serves 4

Note: If you are going to prepare the pears quite some time ahead, leave the quartered pears in a pint of water mixed with the juice of half a lemon until you are ready to use them. This will keep the pears from turning color.

ASPARACADO WHEELS

4 slices white bread
8 short-stemmed
  asparagus spears
1 large avocado
1/4 cup mayonnaise
  Juice of 1/4 lemon

1 tablespoon white wine
1/2 teaspoon caraway
  seeds
  Salt
  White pepper

*T*rim off the bread crusts. Lay the slices out on a board and roll them flat with a rolling pin, but not so thin as to tear them. Steam the asparagus, then let cool. Peel the avocado and remove the pit. Cut the avocado into medium-thin slices. Mix the mayonnaise, lemon juice, wine, caraway seeds, and salt and pepper to taste. Spread this mixture on the bread. Place an asparagus spear at each end, the stem in the middle. Place avocado slices on the asparagus spears. Roll up and chill. To serve, cut into 1/2- to 1-inch slices.
  Serves 4

FRIED CHEESE

12   strips firm cheese
    (such as mozzarella),
    each 3/4 inch wide
    and 4 to 5 inches
    long

1   cup flour
2   eggs, beaten well
    Italian seasoned bread
    crumbs
    Oil

*R*oll the cheese in flour; dip in the eggs and then the bread crumbs. Fry in at least 1 inch of oil in a large skillet until golden brown. Serve 3 per person. A nice dry wine goes well with this.
    Serves 4

If you like, you can do this with zucchini sticks as well.

DOLMATHES

24   fresh grapevine
    leaves
1   pound lamb, finely
    chopped
1/2   cup raw rice,
    washed and dried
1   medium onion,
    finely grated
3 to 4   tablespoons pine
    nuts

4   tablespoons
    creamed corn
2   tablespoons fresh
    dill
4   tablespoons
    chopped fresh
    parsley
    Salt
    Pepper

Egg-Lemon Sauce

2   eggs
6   tablespoons lemon
    juice

1   teaspoon arrowroot
    powder

*B*lanch the leaves in boiling water for 1 to 2 minutes. Drain them and set aside. Mix the lamb, rice, onion, pine nuts, corn, dill, parsley, salt, and pepper. Line the bottom and sides of a buttered large pan with a few of the leaves. Trim the stalk off the remaining leaves and fill each from the large end with stuffing; fold the stem over, tuck in the sides, and roll into a shape resembling a large sausage. Place the end of the leaf underneath and lay an object of some sort on the top of them to hold them together. Pour 1 to 2 pints hot water over them. Cover the pan, place in a 375° oven, and bake for about 1 hour.

Remove from the oven and drain the liquid carefully from the pan. Beat the eggs with the lemon juice. Add the arrowroot, mixed with a bit of warm water, and beat well. Pour over the stuffed grape leaves and put the pan on the stove over low heat; simmer for about 5 minutes, but do not let it come to a boil at any time. Once the leaves have incorporated the sauce, you can serve them, 4 per person.

Serves 6

CAPONATA

4	tablespoons olive oil	$1/2$	cup chopped celery
1	eggplant, with the skin left on, cut into small cubes	$1/2$	cup chopped green and black olives
1	finely chopped onion	$1/2$	cup chopped tomatoes
2	garlic cloves, finely chopped	$1/8$	teaspoon sugar
2	tablespoons minced fennel (*not* fennel seeds)	2	tablespoons red wine vinegar
		2	tablespoons capers
			Salt
			Black pepper

*H*eat the oil in a large skillet. Add the eggplant and sauté to a light golden color. Remove from the skillet and drain well. Sauté the onion, garlic, fennel, and celery, and add the remaining ingredients. Cook until the celery is soft. Add the eggplant and cook until it is rather soft. Serve chilled or just cooled, with garlic bread or regular Italian bread.

Serves 4

QUESO

4	tablespoons oil	1	pound Monterey Jack cheese
1	yellow onion, finely chopped	1/2	cup heavy cream
1/2	cup finely chopped green pepper	8	flour or corn tortillas, toasted
1/2	pound thinly sliced mushrooms		

*H*eat oil in a large skillet. Sauté the onion and pepper. Add the mushrooms and cook until done. In a double boiler, melt the cheese slowly. Mix in the cream. Add the mushroom mixture and blend well. Spoon the mixture onto the tortillas and serve, 2 per person.

Serves 4

SOUPS

There is so much to be said for soups—they can be served with classical dinners, for guests on special occasions, or just for plain meals.

No matter what kind of soups you make, *no* soup that has cream or any type of pasta in it can be frozen. The reason is quite simple: cream curdles when thawed, and pasta turns to mush. Nor should fruit soups be frozen. Also, most soups should not be kept for more than two or three days, refrigerated.

I have listed servings per recipe, but this can vary greatly, depending on whether it is being served as a first course or a full one.

Cold Soups

COLD CREAM OF TOMATO SOUP

3 cups fresh tomatoes, cut into small pieces	3 tablespoons flour
1 small onion, coarsely chopped	3 tablespoons butter
Small pinch of ground cloves	3 cups cream or half-and-half
1/2 cup water	Salt
	White pepper
	Chopped fresh parsley

*P*ut the tomatoes, onion, cloves, and water in a large pot and bring to a boil. Simmer for at least 20 minutes. Remove to a food processor, purée it, and set it aside. Make a roux by cooking the flour in the butter for about 6 to 8 minutes over a low flame. Do not let it get dark. When it is done, begin adding the cream, a bit at a time, until it becomes a rather thick cream sauce (a béchamel). Combine it with the tomato mixture and just heat through. Add salt and pepper to taste. Chill well, and serve with a large sprinkling of parsley on top.

Serves 6

COLD CHICKEN SOUP

3 large scallions	12 to 16 ounces cooked chicken meat, cut into julienne 1/2 inch thick
Butter	
4 cups chicken stock	
1 cup light beer	6 slices hard-boiled egg
White pepper	

*C*hop the scallions into small pieces and place in a small pan. Add a small amount of butter, set in a 360° oven, and bake for about 10 minutes. Remove and set aside.

Heat the chicken stock and add the beer and pepper. Let it

simmer for 10 to 12 minutes, then add the chicken to heat through. Refrigerate until cooled, then remove the chicken strips. Add the scallions to the stock and purée the stock in a food processor or blender. Add the chicken to it again and check for seasoning. Serve in cold soup cups with egg slices for garnish.

Serves 6

This soup comes from Russia, where it is called okrushka.

CHILLED ALMOND SOUP

1/3	cup blanched almonds	2	cups heavy cream
2	scallions, white part only		Dash of mace
			Salt
1	small celery stalk		White pepper
2	cups chicken stock		Chopped fresh parsley

*F*inely grind together the almonds, scallions, and celery. Heat the chicken stock and add the ground mixture. Simmer for at least a half hour. Force through a fine sieve, then add the cream and seasonings to taste, being careful not to add too much mace. Chill, and serve topped with parsley.

Serves 4

COLD EAST INDIAN SOUP

2	small onions, minced	2	fresh tomatoes, chopped
1	tablespoon butter		
1	garlic clove	2	tablespoons grated coconut
1/2	teaspoon curry powder		
1	tablespoon flour	1	teaspoon lemon juice
1	quart chicken stock	1	pint heavy cream
1	sour green apple, cored and finely chopped		

Slightly brown the onions in the butter. Add the garlic, curry powder, and flour. Cook for several minutes. Add the chicken stock, apple, tomatoes, coconut, and lemon juice, and simmer, covered, for 2 hours. Strain and cool. Blend in the cream just before serving.

Serves 4

ROMANOFF'S SENEGALESE SOUP

4	cups chicken stock	2	egg yolks
2	tablespoons butter	1	cup heavy cream
1 1/2	tablespoons curry powder	1	small avocado, diced

Heat the chicken stock, add the butter and curry powder, and blend well. Beat the egg yolks, mix with the cream, and stir into the chicken stock. Simmer very slowly until it becomes somewhat thick. Chill well and garnish with avocado.

Serves 4

TANABOUN

2	onions, finely minced	2	cups clarified chicken stock
2	celery stalks, finely minced	1	pint plain yogurt
4	tablespoons melted butter	2	jiggers semisweet white wine
1	pint sour cream		White pepper
			Paprika

Sauté the minced onion and celery in the butter until soft. Put all of the ingredients, except paprika, in a food processor or blender and purée them. Pour the purée into a pot, heat to a simmer, and let it simmer for 5 minutes. Remove from the pot, chill, and serve with a sprinkling of paprika on top.

Serves 6

BORSCHT

1	pint beef stock	2	tablespoons sugar
1	pint canned tomatoes	1	tablespoon paprika
1	large onion, minced	4	parsley sprigs
1	garlic clove, minced	1/4	teaspoon salt
2	16-ounce cans sliced beets		Pepper
1	bay leaf	6	tablespoons sour cream

*P*ut the stock, tomatoes, onion, and garlic in a pot and bring to a boil. When the onion is soft, add the remaining ingredients except sour cream, and simmer for 1 hour. Remove the bay leaf. Force the soup through a sieve, then chill it. Serve in chilled soup cups, with a large tablespoon of sour cream on top of each.

Serves 6

BORSCHT, POLISH STYLE

3/4	pound canned sliced beets	1	tablespoon lemon juice
2	tablespoons chopped onion		Salt
1/2	cup vinegar		Pepper
1	tablespoon sugar	2	tablespoons sour cream
1 1/2	pints water		

*D*rain the beets. Put the beet juice, onion, vinegar, sugar, and 1 pint water in a large soup pot. Simmer until the onion is cooked. Chop or dice the beets. When the onion is done, add the rest of the water and the beets and lemon juice. Bring to a boil, then check for seasoning. Remove from the heat and let cool.

Serves 6

If you add the vinegar a bit at a time, the soup will come out just the way you like it. Do not follow this or any other recipe word for word and by the exact measurements; season a bit at a time to reach your own final taste-goal.

BORSCHT, RUSSIAN STYLE

1½	quarts beef stock	2	tablespoons parsley sprigs
½	cup canned tomatoes	1	tablespoon sugar
2	tablespoons diced onion	¼	teaspoon paprika
⅛	teaspoon minced garlic	½	bay leaf
¾	pound canned beets, with juice	⅜	teaspoon salt
¼	cup lemon juice		Pepper
			Sour cream

*P*ut the beef stock, tomatoes, onion, and garlic in a stockpot and simmer until the onion is done. Add the remaining ingredients, except sour cream, and simmer for 1½ hours. Strain the soup through a large china cap, forcing through as much of the pulp as you can. Serve cold or hot, garnished with sour cream.
Serves 6

CHILLED PLUM SOUP

1	pound plums, pitted	8	cups water
6	tablespoons sugar	2	jiggers plum wine
	Zest of ½ lemon	5	whole cloves

*P*ut all of the ingredients in a pot and bring to a boil. Turn the flame down and simmer until the fruit is very soft. Remove the lemon zest and cloves, purée the plums, and refrigerate the soup until chilled.
Serves 6 to 8

Serve this sweet soup garnished with a small lemon cookie or a piece of angel food cake.

MELON CREAM SOUP

2 large ripe honeydew
   melons (about 3
   pounds each)
1 cup heavy cream
4 tablespoons port
4 teaspoons finely
   chopped mint

1 small cucumber, peeled,
   cut in half
   lengthwise, seeded,
   and very thinly sliced
Mint sprigs

*C*ut the melons in half and scrape out the seeds and strings. Scoop out the flesh and purée it in a food processor or blender. Strain through a fine sieve into a large bowl. You should have about 6 cups. Add the cream, port, and chopped mint. Refrigerate, covered, for at least an hour before serving. In serving bowls or a tureen, float thin slices of cucumber on the soup, and garnish with mint sprigs.

Serves 6

COLD PEACH SOUP

5 large ripe peaches,
   peeled and
   quartered
3 to 4 tablespoons sugar
1/4 cup sour cream
1/4 cup fresh lemon
   juice

1/4 cup sweet sherry
2 tablespoons thawed
   orange juice
   concentrate
Fresh peaches,
   peeled and sliced

*P*urée the quartered peaches with sugar in a food processor or blender. Mix in the sour cream. Add the lemon juice, sherry, and orange juice, and blend until smooth. Transfer to a bowl, cover, and refrigerate until well chilled. Ladle the soup into bowls. Garnish each bowl with peach slices and serve.

Serves 6 to 8

Hot Soups

*T*here are four ways to make stock: from the natural product itself (meat, chicken, etc.), from a good base, from liquid purchased in a can, and from a bouillon cube. There is never quite enough time for the average person to do it from scratch, so I suggest a base. The L. J. Minor Corp. of Cleveland, Ohio, sells excellent bases for soups and sauces; to order, call 1 (800) 441-5914. Purchase one for, say, chicken. Boil the amount of water for the amount of soup you wish to make (for two people, 1 quart). Add some of the base to the water, and keep tasting until it reaches the flavor you desire. You now have the stock for the soup. Do you wish to make a chicken rice soup? Fine— just add some chopped, diced, or even ground-up chicken and a bit of chopped or ground onion, carrot, and celery. (This is called a mirepoix, used to make the soup stock rich with an abundance of flavor.) Cook this in the stock, add cooked rice, season with salt and pepper, and you are done.

Once you have chicken stock you can make soups of many varieties. For example, buy broccoli or cauliflower. Cut off the stems, finely chop them, and sauté them in butter. Simmer the florets in a pot of chicken stock until soft. Add the sautéed stems and season to taste. *Voilà!*

But perhaps you want to make cream of broccoli soup. Make a béchamel: take cream, half-and-half, milk, or even skim milk, and thicken it with a roux. A roux is nothing more than equal parts of flour and butter cooked together over a medium to low flame for 5 to 10 minutes. (Stir it often to keep it from getting too dark.) Add the béchamel to the clear broccoli soup and you have cream of broccoli soup. It is as easy as that!

CHICKEN STOCK

1	5-pound chicken, cut up	2	celery stalks, chopped
2	carrots, peeled and chopped	1	onion, peeled and chopped
		12	parsley sprigs

*P*ut all of the ingredients in a pot and cover with water. Bring to a boil, then simmer for 2 hours. Skim the fat from the stock. Remove the chicken. (Use it for a garnish in chicken soup, or for chicken salad.) Strain the stock through cheesecloth and let cool.

Makes approximately 5 quarts

OSUIMONO SOUP

6	cups chicken stock	1¹/₂	cups diced cooked chicken
1¹/₂	teaspoons light soy sauce	2	scallions, finely chopped
1	teaspoon sugar	4	parsley sprigs
¹/₂	teaspoon salt		

*C*ombine the chicken stock, soy sauce, sugar, and salt and bring to a boil. Set on simmer, and mix in the chicken and scallions. Serve garnished with parsley sprigs.

Serves 4

FRENCH ONION SOUP

3	medium to large onions	1	tablespoon each port and sherry
8	tablespoons (1 stick) butter		Salt
2	cups chicken stock		Pepper
2	cups beef stock	5	slices French bread
		5	slices mozzarella cheese

*C*ut each onion in half lengthwise. Cut across into slices about 1/8 inch thick. Sauté them in butter for a few minutes, then put a cover on the pot, lower the heat, and cook for 5 to 10 minutes. Uncover, add the stocks, and bring to a boil. Lower the heat and simmer for 5 minutes. Add the wines and seasoning and simmer for about 20 minutes.

Lightly butter the bread, cover with slices of cheese, and bake until slightly browned but not too crusty. Remove, let cool, and cut into bite-size pieces. Put about 12 to 14 pieces in each bowl and pour on the soup.

Serves 5

CREOLE-STYLE ONION SOUP

6	large onions	1/8	teaspoon allspice
1	medium turnip	11/2	cups soft bread crumbs
1/2	medium head white celery		Milk
8	tablespoons (1 stick) butter		Salt
			Pepper
3	cups boiling water	1	egg yolk
1/2	tablespoon anchovy paste or mashed fillets		Minced fresh parsley or croutons or sautéed slices of French bread
1	blade mace		

*C*hop the onions, turnip, and celery. Melt the butter in a large skillet and add the vegetables. Cook over moderate heat, stirring frequently, until golden brown. Do not let them burn. Turn them into a stockpot, along with any butter remaining in the pan. Add the boiling water, anchovy paste, mace, and allspice. Simmer until the vegetables are tender. Purée them together through a sieve. Return them to the stock (discarding the mace) and cook over low heat for 30 minutes. Moisten the bread crumbs with a little milk and mash to a paste. Add to the soup and blend. Correct the seasoning with salt and pepper (or more anchovy paste, if desired). Cook gently for 10 to 15 minutes.

Beat the egg yolk, and heat it by adding a spoonful of the hot soup. Pour the mixture slowly into the soup and blend. Cook for 3 to 4 minutes, stirring constantly. Serve with parsley, croutons, or bread slices.

Serves 4 to 5

VEGETABLE BEEF SOUP

1 pound lean beef, cut into 1/2-inch dice	1/2 cup diced potato
1 cup mirepoix (chopped celery, carrots, and onions)	1 cup cooked mixed vegetables (may use leftovers)
2 tablespoons oil	1/2 cup chopped tomatoes
2 bay leaves	Salt
1 quart beef stock	Pepper

Sauté the beef and mirepoix in oil. Add the bay leaves and beef stock and bring to boil. Add the potato and cook until done. Add the vegetables and tomatoes and heat through. Adjust the seasoning and serve.

Serves 4

POTAGE DUCHESSE

1/3 cup finely chopped carrots	2 tablespoons flour
3/8 cup finely chopped celery	1 3/4 cups milk
2 teaspoons finely chopped onion	1 3/4 cups chicken stock
3 to 3 1/2 tablespoons butter	5 ounces sharp cheddar cheese
	Chopped fresh parsley

Simmer the carrots and celery in 1 cup water until tender, about 15 minutes. Sauté the onion in butter until soft but not browned. Add the flour and blend well. Set the pan over hot water, add the milk and chicken stock, and cook until thickened, stirring constantly. Add the cheese and stir until blended. Add the cooked vegetables and their cooking water and heat thoroughly. Serve garnished with parsley.

Serves 5

RHODE ISLAND CLAM CHOWDER

2	large onions, cut into 1/2-inch dice	6	large quahogs or 10 large clams, chopped
8	ounces salt pork, cut into 1/2-inch dice	12	ounces clam juice
			Salt
3	large potatoes, peeled, blanched, and cut into 1/2-inch dice		Pepper

*S*auté the onions in salt pork until translucent. Bring 2 quarts water to a boil, then reduce the heat and simmer the potatoes, clams, and clam juice for 6 to 8 minutes. Season to taste and serve.

Serves 4; makes 2 quarts

Variation: New England Clam Chowder. Add cream or béchamel sauce; it should be served slightly thick.

MANHATTAN CLAM CHOWDER

1	quart Rhode Island clam chowder	8	ounces canned tomatoes, (with juice), cut into 1-inch dice
1	celery stalk, cut into 1-inch dice		
1	leek, cut into 1-inch dice	1/2	tablespoon crushed garlic
1/2	green pepper, seeded and cut into 1-inch dice	1/2	teaspoon thyme
		1/2	teaspoon rosemary
			Butter

*H*eat up the chowder. Sauté the vegetables and herbs. Add to the chowder, season to taste, and serve.
Serves 4

SEAFOOD GUMBO FILÉ

4	tablespoons butter	1	pound small shrimp, peeled and deveined
3 to 4	tablespoons flour		
1	celery stalk, chopped	1/2	pound fish, flaked
			Salt
1	small onion, chopped		Pepper
1	garlic clove, chopped	8	ounces frozen or canned okra, chopped
1	12-ounce can tomatoes	1/2	teaspoon filé

*M*ake a roux with the butter and flour. When it is cooked, add the celery, onion, and garlic, and cook until tender. Add the tomatoes and 2 tomato cans of water. Add the shrimp and fish. Season to taste and simmer until done. Then add the okra. When you are ready to serve the soup, sprinkle filé on the bowl or cup of gumbo.
Serves 4
Note: If you use fresh okra, add it early enough so it can cook for 10 to 12 minutes.

A soup that is a meal in itself.

CHICKEN AND SHRIMP GUMBO FILÉ

1	4-pound chicken, cut into pieces	1/4	pound salt pork, diced
1	garlic clove	1	sweet red pepper, seeded and cut up
	Salt		
	Pepper	1	cup chopped onions

1/2   cup flour
21/2 cups (1 1-pound
      3-ounce can)
      tomatoes
1   10-ounce package
      frozen okra, thawed

1   pound shrimp, peeled
      and deveined
      Hot pepper sauce
2   teaspoons gumbo filé
      powder
      Hot cooked rice

Cook the chicken with 5 cups water, the garlic, 1 tablespoon salt, and 1/4 teaspoon pepper for 30 minutes, or until tender. Let cool and remove the meat from the bones; cut into pieces. Strain the stock, add enough water to make 6 cups, let cool, and skim off the fat. Cook the salt pork until well browned. Remove it from the kettle and pour off all but 1/4 cup fat. Sauté the red pepper and onions in the fat for 5 minutes. Add the flour and brown it. Gradually stir in the stock. Add the salt pork and tomatoes, cover, and simmer for 30 minutes. Add the chicken, okra, and shrimp. Simmer, covered, until the shrimp turn pink. Season with salt, pepper, and hot pepper sauce. Gradually add the filé powder, and stir until completely blended. Put a scoop of rice in each soup bowl and fill with gumbo filé.

Serves 6

CHICKEN AND OKRA GUMBO

1   3-pound frying
      chicken, cut up
2   tablespoons lard or
      butter
1   pound smoked ham,
      cut into 1/2-inch dice
1   onion, chopped
6   large fresh tomatoes,
      peeled and chopped
2   pints okra, sliced 1/2
      inch thick

      Salt
      Cayenne pepper
      Few parsley sprigs,
      chopped
1   bay leaf
1   pod dried red pepper,
      without seeds
6   cups water
12   shucked oysters
      Hot cooked rice

Cut the chicken into 12 pieces. Heat lard in a heavy kettle. Add the chicken and ham. Cover and cook slowly for 10 minutes. Add the onion, tomatoes, and okra. Cook, stirring, over high heat for 4 to 5 minutes. Season with salt and cayenne. Add parsley, bay leaf, red pepper, and water. Bring to a boil, cover, and simmer for 1 1/2 to 2 hours. Add the oysters and cook for a few minutes. Add more salt and cayenne, if necessary. Serve with rice.

Serves 6 to 8

CREOLE BOUILLABAISSE

1	tablespoon butter	1/2	teaspoon salt
	Flour	1 3/4	cups canned tomatoes
1	onion, chopped	1/2	cup water
1	garlic clove, minced	1	pound red snapper, cut into small pieces
1	teaspoon curry powder		
	Dash of hot pepper sauce	1	pound redfish, cut into small pieces
4	whole cloves	1/4	cup sherry
1	bay leaf	2	ounces (1/2 4-ounce can) mushroom caps, undrained
1/4	teaspoon crumbled dried thyme		

Melt the butter in a skillet. Add the flour and cook over low heat until golden brown, stirring constantly. Add the onion and garlic; continue cooking for 2 to 3 minutes. Add the curry powder, hot pepper sauce, half of the cloves, half of the bay leaf, and the thyme and salt. After a minute or two, add the tomatoes and water. Simmer slowly, covered, for 30 minutes.

Put the fish in another skillet. Cover with boiling water; add the remaining cloves and bay leaf and half of the sherry. Lower the heat and simmer gently for 8 minutes; drain. Put the fish and mushrooms in the sauce and heat for 5 minutes. Add the remaining sherry and serve.

Serves 6

Cooking the seasonings in a roux gives this dish a very special flavor.

CRAB SOUP WITH TOMATOES AND GARLIC

4 or 5	hard-shell crabs, plus the meat from 5 more crabs	1/4	teaspoon dried thyme	
2	quarts water	1	bay leaf	
2	tablespoons lard		Salt	
1	large onion, chopped		Pepper	
4	garlic cloves, minced		Cayenne pepper	
1	rounded tablespoon flour	2	egg yolks	
1	cup peeled and chopped tomatoes	1	rounded tablespoon butter Yolks of hard-boiled eggs	

*B*oil the crabs in water to cover. When they are bright red, drain them and discard the water. Pick over the crab meat and reserve. Put the shells and all the trimmings (except the spongy lungs) in a heavy pot with the 2 quarts water. Bring to a boil and skim. Reduce the heat and simmer for 20 minutes. Strain and reserve the broth.

Melt the lard in a heavy soup kettle. Add the onion and garlic and cook over moderate heat until they are golden, stirring frequently. Add the flour, blend, and let brown. Add the tomatoes and herbs. Cook for 5 minutes, stirring from time to time. Add the reserved broth and the crab meat; reduce the heat to low and simmer for 1 hour. Season to taste with salt, pepper, and cayenne.

Just before serving, beat the raw egg yolks. Add 1 or 2 spoonfuls of the hot soup to them and blend, then slowly stir the mixture into the soup. Cook, stirring constantly, for 3 to 4 minutes. Stir in the butter, garnish with hard-boiled egg yolks, and serve.

Serves 6 to 8

CREAM OF CRAB SOUP

	Yolks of 2 hard-boiled eggs	1	shallot or scallion, minced
4	tablespoons butter	3	cups half-and-half
1	tablespoon flour	2	cups heavy cream
	Grated zest of 1 lemon	2	cups crab meat
1	teaspoon Worcestershire sauce		Salt
			White pepper
1	dash of hot pepper sauce or Tabasco sauce		Cayenne pepper
		2	tablespoons Madeira or sherry, or to taste
1/8	teaspoon mace		

*M*ash the egg yolks in a bowl and blend with 3 tablespoons of the butter and the flour, lemon zest, Worcestershire sauce, hot pepper sauce, and mace. Let stand while you sauté the shallot in the remaining 1 tablespoon butter over low heat. Do not brown it. Heat the half-and-half and cream together in the top of a large double boiler over hot water. Slowly stir in the egg mixture, shallot, and crab meat. Cook for 20 minutes, stirring frequently. Season to taste with salt, pepper, and cayenne. Add the wine just before serving.

Serves 6 to 8

SHRIMP BISQUE

2	cups shrimp stock	8	ounces shrimp, peeled, deveined, and cubed
2	cups half-and-half		
1/4	cup roux (equal parts flour and butter, cooked)	1	tablespoon butter
		1/4	cup sherry
			Salt
1/4	cup mirepoix (chopped celery, carrots, and onions)		Pepper

*C*ombine the shrimp stock and half-and-half; bring to a boil. Thicken with the roux and simmer in the top of a double boiler for 10 minutes. Sauté the mirepoix and shrimp in butter. Add the sherry and reduce by half. Combine the mirepoix and shrimp mixture with the soup. Season to taste, heat through, and serve. Bisques are thick, so add more roux if necessary.

Serves 4

CREAM OF TOMATO SOUP

About 2/3 cup tomato juice	1	tablespoon tomato paste
1	whole peppercorn	1	tablespoon butter
1/4	bay leaf	1	tablespoon flour
1	thin slice onion	1/4	teaspoon salt
		1/2	cup milk

*S*immer together for 5 minutes the tomato juice, peppercorn, bay leaf, and onion, then strain into a glass measuring cup. Add enough tomato juice to bring the volume to 2/3 cup; add the tomato paste and blend.

Make a white sauce by melting the butter in a saucepan, adding flour and salt, and blending until smooth; add the milk gradually, off the heat, constantly stirring to form a smooth paste. Bring the mixture to a boil, stirring constantly. Add the tomato juice mixture and heat to serving temperature, but do not let it boil.

Serves 2

CHEDDAR CHEESE SOUP

1	quart chicken stock	1	pound cheddar cheese, grated
1	quart half-and-half		Salt
1/2	cup roux (equal parts flour and butter, cooked)		Pepper

*C*ombine the chicken stock and half-and-half; bring to a boil. Thicken with the roux and simmer in the top of a double boiler

for 10 minutes. Blend in the cheese. Adjust the seasoning and serve.
Serves 4

Variation: Peanut Butter Soup. Substitute peanut butter for the cheese.

DRIED PEA SOUP PAGO PAGO

2	ounces dried green peas	1	tablespoon grated orange zest
2 to 3	tablespoons orange juice	3/4	cup milk
1/4	teaspoon ground mace	2	cups water
		1/2	cup popped popcorn

Combine all of the ingredients, except the popcorn, in a 2-quart saucepan and mix well. Cook, uncovered, over medium heat for 15 minutes, stirring occasionally. Serve at once, in mugs or soup bowls, and top with popcorn.
Serves 4

MEAT

Beef

BEEF WELLINGTON

4	6- to 8-ounce pieces of tenderloin
1	pound mushrooms, very finely chopped or grated
	Melted butter
2	medium onions or 8 shallots, chopped
	Salt
	Pepper
	Lemon juice
1/4	cup chopped fresh parsley
8	phyllo leaves
1	egg, beaten

*S*auté the tenderloin and let cool. Wrap the mushrooms in a towel and squeeze out the excess liquid. Heat some butter in a saucepan and sauté the onions until lightly browned. Add the mushrooms, salt, pepper, and a few drops of lemon juice, and stir over high heat until all moisture has evaporated. Stir in the parsley and let cool.

Place a phyllo leaf on a damp cloth and brush with melted butter. Place a second leaf over the first. Place one tenderloin in the middle of the dough and spread the mushroom mixture over the top of the fillet. Fold a side of dough over half the fillet, and fold the opposite side over to meet it. Fold the remaining sides under, and brush the top with cold water. Repeat with the other fillets and phyllo. Place all on a cookie sheet, seams down. Brush with egg wash, and bake in a preheated oven at 375° for 15 to 20 minutes, or until golden.

Serves 4

Variation: Substitute pâté de foie gras for the mushroom mixture.

STUFFED TENDERLOIN

2¹/2 pounds center cut of
      beef tenderloin
1   cup thinly sliced
      green and red
      peppers
¹/2   cup thinly sliced
      mushrooms

¹/2   cup thinly sliced
      onion
2   tablespoons crushed
      peppercorns
2   pork sausages,
      blanched and sliced
      lengthwise
      Oil

*H*ave the tenderloin cut to resemble a jelly roll or bracciole. On it place a layer of peppers, a layer of mushrooms, and a layer of onion. Sprinkle with peppercorns. Place the sausages on the mixture. Roll up the tenderloin as you would a jelly roll, and secure with toothpicks. Rub with oil and roast at 250° for 30 minutes for medium rare. Remove the toothpicks and slice. Serve on a Madeira brown sauce (page 247).

Serves 4 to 6

CARPETBAGGER

4 8-ounce tenderloin
   steaks

8 large oysters, shucked
4 slices bacon

*C*ut a pocket in each steak. Stuff 2 oysters into each pocket. Wrap each steak with bacon and secure with a toothpick. Broil for approximately 5 minutes on each side for medium rare and to crisp the bacon.

Serves 4

TOURNEDOS ROSSINI

4	9- to 10-ounce tenderloin fillets	2	tablespoons Madeira
	Demiglaze sauce (available from L. J. Minor Corp.)	4	slices goose liver
		4	mushroom caps, trimmed (see note) and sautéed in butter

Slice the fillets in half and cook to order. Mix the demiglaze sauce and Madeira to the desired consistency. Put some of the sauce on each dinner plate. Place the tenderloin on the sauce, and put a slice of goose liver on each slice, topped with just a dab of sauce. Then top with a mushroom cap.

Serves 4

Note: Flute the mushroom caps decoratively: draw a knife at an angle from the top of the center of the mushroom to the bottom, slicing out a piece at an angle. If you want to get fancy, you can cut the initial of each guest on the top of the mushroom.

MEDALLIONS OF TENDERLOIN JOSEPH

4	8- to 10-ounce tenderloins		Demiglaze sauce (available from L. J. Minor Corp.)
	Béarnaise sauce (page 246)	8	asparagus spears
		4	cherry tomatoes

Slice the tenderloins in half. Cook to your preference. Place béarnaise sauce on half of the dinner plate, demiglaze sauce on the other half. Put one piece of meat on each of the sauces. Set 2 spears of asparagus and a cherry tomato in the very center of the plate.

Serves 4

Tenderloin is by far the most tender of all meats, but what do you do when you can't afford this cut? Did you know that you can make a piece of chuck almost as tender as tenderloin? Simply marinate it in papaya or pineapple juice for an hour or more—even overnight, if you have the time. Believe me, it will not alter the taste, and will be good for you as well. If you are unable to buy either of those two juices, use lemon juice, but rinse off the meat before you cook it.

MINI BOULAGE

Marinade

1 tablespoon sweet basil	1 tablespoon Worcestershire sauce
1 tablespoon oregano	
1/4 teaspoon each salt and pepper	1 tablespoon red wine vinegar
1 cup olive oil	1/2 cup Burgundy
4 4-ounce tenderloin steaks	1/2 cup quartered cherry tomatoes
1 cup quartered mushrooms	1/2 cup sliced green peppers

Combine all the dry ingredients of the marinade. Add all the liquid ingredients and mix. Pour the marinade over the steaks and vegetables and marinate for 24 hours.

Bring the marinade and vegetables to a boil in a pan. Add the steaks and cook for 3 minutes on each side for medium rare. Remove the steaks to a platter and reduce the liquid. Pour the liquid and vegetables over the steaks.

Serves 4

PRIME RIB AU JUS

3- or 4-rib roast	Pepper
Salt	Garlic powder

Mirepoix (chopped celery, carrots, and onions)
Beef base (optional; available from L. J. Minor Corp.)
Sherry (optional)

*R*ub the fat side of the rib roast with salt, pepper, and garlic powder. Place the roast on the mirepoix in a roasting pan, rib side down, add a little water for gravy, and bake in a preheated oven at 450° for 15 minutes. Turn the heat down to 325° and finish roasting to your taste (see note). Strain the fat drippings from the pan before you deglaze it, and if there is not enough gravy, add some beef base and a bit of sherry to stretch it. Slice the roast and serve with Yorkshire pudding and horseradish sauce (recipes follow).
Serves 4 to 8

Note: For rare, roast for approximately 11 minutes per pound, or to an interior temperature of 125°; for medium, approximately 12 minutes per pound, or 140°; for well done, approximately 13 minutes per pound, or 150°.

YORKSHIRE PUDDING

1¹/₂	cups flour	4	eggs
¹/₂	teaspoon pepper	1¹/₂	cups milk
1	teaspoon nutmeg	2	cups fat drippings
1	teaspoon salt		from roasting pan

*C*ombine all of the dry ingredients and mix well. Beat the eggs and milk and mix in the dry ingredients. (This can be done in a food processor.) Blend until smooth. Cover and refrigerate for 2 hours.

Preheat the oven to 450°. Use a muffin tin and fill each compartment one third full of fat drippings. Set the tin in the oven. Remove the batter from the refrigerator and beat again to ensure smoothness. When the fat smokes, add the batter to the muffin tin, filling it no more than two thirds full. Bake for 15 minutes at 450°; then reduce the heat to 300° and bake for another 15 minutes. Do not open the oven door until the pudding is done, or it will fall.
Serves 8

HORSERADISH SAUCE

1 cup heavy cream or crème fraîche	4 tablespoons grated fresh horseradish, or 8 tablespoons prepared horseradish
1 tablespoon lemon juice	
1 tablespoon chopped fresh parsley	Salt
	Pepper

*B*eat the cream to the soft-peaks stage. Add the remaining ingredients. Adjust the seasoning and serve.
Serves 4 to 8

Variation: Add 1 or 2 dashes of Worcestershire sauce.

BAKED RIBS OF BEEF DIJONNAISE

2 tablespoons minced garlic	3 tablespoons melted butter
2 tablespoons chopped fresh parsley	Dijon mustard
1 tablespoon pepper	7 ribs from cooked rib roast
	3 cups bread crumbs

*C*ombine the garlic, parsley, pepper, and butter. Spread mustard on the ribs and coat with bread crumbs. Bake in a preheated 375° oven until golden brown.
Serves 7 as an appetizer

RED FLANNEL HASH

2 eggs beaten with 1/4 cup milk	2 tablespoons chopped fresh parsley
Salt	2 pounds beef trimmings, finely chopped
Pepper	

2 potatoes, peeled, blanched, and cut into 1/2-inch dice	2 beets, peeled, blanched, and cut into 1/2-inch dice
1 onion, cut into 1/2-inch dice and briefly sautéed	

Combine the egg mixture with salt, pepper, and parsley. Add the remaining ingredients and combine well. Form into patties and fry in a heavy skillet until browned on both sides and thoroughly heated. Serve plain or with poached or fried eggs.
Serves 8

HOT STEAK SALAD

Marinade

Salt	2 pinches of oregano
Pepper	2 tablespoons red or white vinegar
2 large pinches of minced fresh sweet basil	2 tablespoons olive oil
2 dashes of Worcestershire sauce	4 tablespoons red wine

12 ounces beef tips, thinly sliced, 2 to 3 inches long and 1/2 inch thick	Lettuce Broccoli and cauliflower florets

Dipping Sauce

3 to 4 tablespoons mayonnaise	2 teaspoons minced fresh parsley
4 drops lemon juice	2 to 3 teaspoons dry white wine
2 teaspoons minced onion	Several dashes of dried dill

*C*ombine the marinade ingredients. Marinate the beef tips and cook them in the marinade. Remove and serve on a bed of lettuce with raw cauliflower and broccoli florets on the side.

Whip together the ingredients for the dipping sauce. Pour into a bowl and set in the center of the dish you are serving the steak on. You can also use the marinade as a dipping sauce.

Serves 2

This is an unusual salad—a steak salad served hot, with pieces of fresh vegetables and a special sauce for the vegetables, along with the sauce the dish itself makes.

GRILLADES

1¹/2	pounds round steak, cut ¹/2 inch thick	1	onion, sliced
	Salt	1	garlic clove, minced
	Pepper	1	tomato, chopped
1	tablespoon lard		Parsley sprigs

*C*ut the meat into 4 squares or serving pieces. Season it with salt and pepper, rubbing them in thoroughly. Heat the lard in a heavy skillet and cook the onion and garlic until golden. Add the tomato and steak. Cover and cook slowly, turning occasionally, until brown and tender. Serve garnished with parsley.

Serves 4

THE HIDDEN-CHEESE BURGER

1	pound ground chuck	2	tablespoons steak sauce
	Salt	¹/4	pound grated cheese (your choice)
	Pepper		
2	tablespoons finely chopped fresh parsley		

*M*ix the chuck, salt, pepper, parsley, and steak sauce. Form thick patties, then make a hole in each with your thumb. Fill the hole with cheese and cover with additional meat mixture. Reshape the patty, and fry to the desired doneness. Covering the pan will create steam and help keep your burger moist, and also melt the cheese.

Serves 4

ITALIAN MEATBALLS

	Salt	1	onion, finely minced
	Pepper	1	egg, beaten
1/2	cup cream	2	garlic cloves, finely minced
1	tablespoon finely minced fresh parsley		Bread crumbs, as needed
1	tablespoon finely minced fresh basil	1	pound ground chuck
2	tablespoons grated Parmesan cheese		Olive oil

*C*ombine the salt, pepper, cream, parsley, basil, cheese, onion, egg, garlic, and bread crumbs. Blend thoroughly. Add the chuck and mix together. Form into 16 meatballs. Fry slowly in olive oil until done.

Serves 4

MEAT LOAF WITH DILL AND HARD-BOILED EGGS

1	egg, beaten	2	tablespoons finely chopped fresh dill
	Salt		
	Pepper	2	pounds ground chuck
2	tablespoons Worcestershire sauce	3	eggs, hard-boiled and peeled
1	cup half-and-half	8	strips bacon
1/4	cup bread crumbs		

Combine the beaten egg, salt, pepper, Worcestershire sauce, half-and-half, bread crumbs, dill, and chuck. Mix thoroughly. Trim the hard-boiled eggs at the ends so that they butt together to form one tubular egg. Shape the meat loaf so that it surrounds the eggs completely. Place the bacon strips over the loaf and tuck the ends under. Poke a few random holes through the bacon to allow steam to escape and bacon fat to drip into the loaf. Bake at 350° for 30 minutes, then at 500° long enough to crisp the bacon.

Serves 6 to 8

REAL SHEPHERD'S PIE

1	pound lean hamburger	4	large potatoes, peeled
1	large onion, finely chopped		Cream or milk
			Butter
1/2	teaspoon poultry seasoning	1	small can corn niblets
	Salt	1	small can baby peas
	Pepper		Paprika

Sauté the hamburger with the onion. Add the poultry seasoning and a bit of salt and pepper to taste. Cook the potatoes. Mash them with some cream or milk and just a bit of butter, if you like. Place the cooked hamburger in the bottom of a 5 × 10-inch casserole, about 2 inches high or even more. Cover half of the meat with corn and the other half with peas. Top with the mashed potatoes and dot with butter. Sprinkle the top with paprika. Bake at 350° until golden brown.

Serves 4

Veal

I feel that something should be said of this youngest and most tender of meats. Veal is the milk-fed meat of calves that are slaughtered no more than 12 weeks after birth. It has very little or no fat at all and a very high moisture content, so it will dry out quickly if left out too long or cooked too long. Even cooking it at too high a temperature is taboo. Veal has a delicate flavor and for this reason blends well with other foods as well as sauces. If cooked properly, veal will always be tender and cook quickly; it will display a fine appearance and texture when served. It is the gentlest of meats. So handle it gently, and the results will always be gratifying.

VEAL SCALLOPS, FRENCH STYLE

8	tablespoons (1 stick) butter		Flour
24	scalloped pieces of pounded veal, about the size of a silver dollar	3	eggs, beaten lightly
			Juice of 2 lemons
		1/2	cup Chablis

*M*elt the butter in a very large saucepan. Warm it gently. Pat the veal in flour. Dip in egg wash. Sauté lightly. Halfway through the first side's cooking, squeeze the lemon juice over the veal pieces. Turn them. Pour the wine over the second side, and finish sautéing the veal for but a few minutes. Remove the veal. Finish the sauce by reducing it just a bit. Pour it over the veal, serving 6 pieces per person.
Serves 4

SALTIMBOCCA

1	cup olive oil		Large amount of sage
4	very large slices veal		Butter
8	slices prosciutto	1/4	cup Madeira
4	large slices mozzarella cheese		

*H*eat the oil in a large skillet. Sauté the veal on one side and remove. Pat each cooked side dry with paper towels and lay prosciutto and cheese on it. Fold the veal over and return it to the hot oil. Sprinkle sage on top of the veal. Sauté for a few minutes and remove. Drain most of the oil from the pan, add butter, heat it, and put the veal back in, cooked side up. Sprinkle sage on top and finish cooking (a few minutes). At the very end, add the wine. Remove the veal and deglaze the skillet. When the sauce is finished, pour it over the veal.
Serves 4

VEAL PAUPIETTES WITH OYSTERS

8	thin slices veal of equal size	1/8	teaspoon pepper
1	cup soft bread crumbs	1/2	pint shucked oysters, with their liquor
1/4	pound lean pork	4	slices bacon
1	tablespoon grated onion		Melted butter
1	tablespoon minced fresh parsley	1/3	cup dry white wine (or more if needed)
1/2	teaspoon salt		Minced fresh parsley for garnish

*H*ave the butcher pound the meat to an even thickness and trim the slices to an even size and shape. Moisten the bread crumbs with cold water and gently squeeze out the excess. Put the pork through the finest blade of a meat grinder and combine with the bread crumbs. Blend the onion, parsley, salt, and pepper thoroughly. Spread a portion of this mixture evenly over each slice of veal. Poach the oysters in their liquor until plump; drain. Chop them and spread over the pork mixture.

Cut the bacon slices in half and lay half a slice crosswise over the oysters at one end of each veal slice. Roll up the slices, starting at the end with the bacon, so that the bacon will be at the middle of each paupiette. Tie the rolls several times around with thread. Brush with melted butter and lay side by side in a shallow baking dish. Brush the tops with more butter, and sprinkle lightly with additional salt and pepper. Bake at 325° for 1 hour, basting with the remaining butter every 10 to 15 minutes. Baste with the pan juices as they accumulate. Add a few tablespoons of hot water to the pan if there are signs of charring. When the veal is done, slip the baking pan under the broiler for 1 to 2 minutes to brown on top. Remove to a heated platter. Place the baking dish on top of the stove over moderate heat. Add the wine and swish it around, scraping up any browned bits. Add a pinch of salt and pepper if necessary, and when the liquid in the pan has been reduced to several spoonfuls, pour it over the paupiettes and sprinkle with minced parsley. Serve immediately.

Serves 4

CASHEWED VEAL BIRDS

4 slices cubed soft bread
1/2 teaspoon crushed
      coriander seeds
1/8 teaspoon curry powder
1/2 cup honey
1/2 teaspoon celery salt
1 cup finely chopped
    cashews

1 cup sauterne
8 slices veal, pounded
    thin
1 cup chicken or veal
    stock
1 cup heavy cream

*M*ix the bread, coriander seeds, curry powder, honey, celery salt, cashews, and most of the wine into a stuffing. Spread evenly on the slices of veal and roll them into a hot-dog shape. Place in a baking pan, moisten with a bit of stock, cover the pan, and bake at 375° for 15 to 20 minutes. Serve 2 stuffed birds on each dinner plate, with a sauce made with the cream, stock, and a bit of wine. Season it to taste with salt and white pepper, if you wish.
Serves 4

VEAL SCALOPPINE MILANESE

Flour
24 pieces of veal (cut into
      2-inch squares)
Mixture of oil and
      butter
1 pound thinly sliced
    mushrooms
2 tablespoons chopped
    fresh parsley

1 cup peeled, seeded,
    diced fresh tomatoes
1/2 cup Marsala
1 garlic clove, pressed
2 tablespoons freshly
    chopped sweet basil
4 tablespoons grated
    Romano cheese

*F*lour the veal and sauté it in the mixture of oil and butter. Mix in the remaining ingredients, place in a large covered casserole dish, and bake in a preheated 375° oven for 15 to 20 minutes. Serve with noodles.
Serves 4

VEAL CARMEN

1	onion, chopped	1/4	teaspoon rosemary
2	shallots, finely chopped		Flour
	Mixture of oil and butter	4	large veal cutlets
			Juice of 1/2 lemon
1	cup sliced mushrooms	1	cup chicken or veal stock
6	tomatoes, peeled, seeded, and chopped	1/4	teaspoon prepared mustard
1/4	cup Chablis		Several slices mozzarella cheese
1	teaspoon tarragon		
1/2	teaspoon sugar		

*S*auté the onion and shallots in the mixture of oil and butter. Add the mushrooms and cook until they begin to change color. Add the tomatoes and simmer for 5 minutes. Add the wine, tarragon, sugar, and rosemary and cook for 15 minutes.

Flour the veal and lightly brown it in the oil-butter mixture in another pan. Remove; add the lemon juice and stock to the pan and reduce it by half. Blend the mustard into the sautéed onion mixture, add the reduced stock, and put in a casserole dish with the veal. Top with the cheese, then bake in a preheated 400° oven for 15 minutes or more, until the cheese melts.

Serves 4

VEAL AND EGGPLANT PARMIGIANA

4	veal cutlets	2	eggplants
	Flour	1	quart spaghetti sauce
4	eggs, slightly beaten	1	cup grated Romano cheese
1	can Italian bread crumbs	8	slices Romano cheese
	Mixture of oil and butter		

*P*ound the veal cutlets until thin. Flour them, dip them in egg wash, then in bread crumbs, and sauté in the mixture of oil and butter until just barely cooked. Slice the eggplants lengthwise, flour them, dip them in egg wash and bread crumbs, and sauté until just lightly browned on each side. In individual oven casserole dishes, place a bit of sauce on the bottom, put slices of the eggplant on it, veal on it, eggplant on the veal, then a bit more sauce, and top with a sprinkling of grated cheese and 2 cheese slices. Bake the casseroles in a preheated 400° oven until the cheese melts and becomes a nice rich golden brown. Place the casserole dishes on small platters and serve. Serve the remaining sauce on the side.

Serves 4

Note: If the casserole dishes are too small to hold the cutlets in one piece, cut them and the eggplants into strips.

VEAL PAPRIKASH

4	tablespoons butter		Pepper
1/2	cup finely chopped onion	1	egg yolk
		1/2	cup sour cream
1	green pepper, very thinly sliced	2	cups cooked veal, cut into small cubes, then flattened
1	tablespoon flour		
1	tablespoon paprika	2	tablespoons minced fresh dill
11/2	cups chicken stock		
1/8	teaspoon sugar	1/4	teaspoon lemon juice
	Salt		

*M*elt the butter, heat slightly, and sauté the onion, then the green pepper, until done. Mix in the flour and paprika and cook slightly. Slowly add the chicken stock, making a sauce. Turn the heat down to a simmer; add the sugar and a bit of salt and pepper. Let this cook for about 10 minutes. Mix the egg yolk and sour cream and stir into the hot sauce, a bit at a time. Do not let it come to a boil. Add the veal and dill, heat it through, then add the lemon juice to the whole thing. Serve over egg noodles.

Serves 4

PORK TENDERLOIN VÉRONIQUE

2 whole pork tenderloins	4 parsley sprigs, finely
Mixture of oil and	chopped
butter	1 cup dry white wine
2 leeks, white part only	1 cup pork stock
2 celery stalks	Roux (equal parts flour
1 parsnip, finely minced	and butter, cooked)
1 small onion, minced	1 very large bunch
	seedless white grapes

Slice the tenderloins into 24 large pieces. Heat the oil and butter mixture in a heated skillet and sauté the pork very lightly, just 1 to 2 minutes on each side. Remove from the pan. Add the leeks, celery, parsnip, onion, parsley, wine, and stock to the pan. Bring to a boil and simmer for at least 10 minutes. Thicken with the roux, checking for seasoning. (If there is any undue sharpness, add a bit of sweet white wine.) Turn off the heat and set the meat in the sauce for a few minutes. Remove the meat, reheat the sauce, and add the grapes, whole or halved. Place the sauce with the grapes on dinner plates. Lay 4 slices of meat, overlapping each other, on each portion of sauce and serve.

Serve 6

PORK CHOW YOK

1 pound pork tenderloin	1 tablespoon dark brown
1 tablespoon dark soy	sugar
sauce	2 eggs, beaten
1 tablespoon hoisin sauce	Flour
2 tablespoons sweet sake	Oil for deep-frying

Cut the meat into thin strips and flatten them. Soak them overnight in a mixture of soy sauce, hoisin sauce, sake, and sugar.

Dip the meat in the egg wash, then the flour, and fry in deep oil. Serve with Graham Kerr's steamed rice (page 136).
Serves 4

BAKED STUFFED PORK CHOPS

1	onion, minced	6	slices bread
6	tablespoons raisins	1/2	teaspoon sage
2	eggs, beaten	6	double-thick pork
2	tablespoons chopped		chops
	fresh parsley	2	tablespoons butter
1/4	cup milk	2	cups pork stock
6	tablespoons chopped		Roux (equal parts flour
	pineapple		and butter, cooked)
2	celery stalks, minced		

*M*ix the onion, raisins, eggs, parsley, milk, pineapple, celery, bread, and sage into a stuffing. If it is too moist, add more bread; if too dry, add a bit of stock. Cut a large pocket into the center of each chop and fill with the stuffing. Melt the butter in a skillet and brown the chops lightly on both sides, then place them in a roasting pan. Put some of the stock in the pan and bake the chops at 350° for an hour or more, basting often. Remove the chops when done. Deglaze the pan on top of the stove and thicken it with the roux. Serve the chops with a generous amount of sauce.
Serves 6

CREOLE PORK CHOPS

12	small (6-ounce) pork	Just enough salad oil
	chops	to cover the bottom
1	cup flour	of a large skillet
	Salt	Creole sauce (page 252)
	Pepper	

*D*redge the chops in a mixture of flour, salt, pepper. Heat a skillet, heat a film of oil in it, and brown the chops on both sides. Put the chops in a large casserole dish, cover with creole sauce, and bake at 325° until the pork is tender. Serve with plain rice.

Serves 6

A HONEY OF A PORK CHOP

	Oil	2	tablespoons dark brown sugar
12	small pork chops		
1/2	cup applesauce	4	ounces light honey
1	tablespoon hoisin sauce	2	jiggers apple liqueur

*H*eat a skillet, heat a little oil in it, and brown the chops on both sides. Remove the chops, add the remaining ingredients, and bring to a simmer. Cook for a few minutes, then remove from the heat. Put the chops in a large casserole dish, cover with the sauce, and bake, covered, at 375° for 30 minutes. Remove the cover and cook at 325° until the chops are tender. Serve the chops with the sauce over them.

Serves 6

MEDALLIONS OF PORK CALVADOS

8	medallions of pork	1	cup heavy cream
1	teaspoon finely minced shallots	1	apple, cored and sliced into rings
1	tablespoon Dijon mustard	1	tablespoon finely chopped fresh parsley
1/2	cup Calvados (apple brandy)		

*S*auté the medallions, remove them, and keep in a warm place. Remove excess fat from the pan and add the shallots, mustard,

and Calvados. Reduce until almost dry. Add the cream and bring to a boil. Add the apple rings and parsley. Reduce until the sauce thickens. Pour over the medallions and serve.
Serves 2

ROAST PORK

1	butt end of pork loin (5 to 6 pounds), ready for roasting	2	cups mirepoix (coarsely chopped celery, carrots, and onions)
6	garlic cloves	2	cups water
	Salt		Roux (equal parts flour
	Pepper		and butter, cooked)

*L*ooking directly down on the roast, cut 6 small pockets and insert the garlic. Sprinkle the roast with salt and pepper. Place the mirepoix and water in a pan and set the roast on it. Cook at 350° for approximately 1 1/2 hours. Strain the juices, deglaze the pan, and mix with the roux for gravy.
Serves 4

SWEET AND SOUR PORK

1	cup vinegar	1	teaspoon chopped or grated ginger root
1	pint sugar		
3 1/2	cups water		
6 to 8	tablespoons cornstarch	1 1/2 to 2	pounds boneless pork, cut into strips 1/2 inch thick and 3 to 4 inches long
1	cup sweet relish		
1 to 2	tablespoons soy sauce		
4	tablespoons rice wine		

*M*ix the vinegar, sugar, and 2 3/4 cups water, put in a pot, and boil for 4 or 5 minutes. Dissolve the cornstarch in the remaining water, add to the pot, and whip until smooth and stiff. Add the relish, soy sauce, and rice wine, stirring constantly with a wooden spoon. Add the ginger, simmer for a short time, then remove from the heat. Add the pork and let it marinate for 10 to 15 minutes. In a wok or large skillet, cook the pork in the marinade. Serve over rice.

Serves 4

PORK TERIYAKI

1	pound cubed pork	1/2	cup shoyu sauce
2	tablespoons brown sugar	2	tablespoons sake
1/2	onion, finely minced	1/2	garlic clove, finely minced

Cut the pork into large cubes and marinate overnight in a sauce made from the other ingredients. Broil the pork slowly on a charcoal grill, basting and turning as often as seems necessary. Serve with rice.

Serves 4

PORK KNUCKLES IN SAUCE

4	pork knuckles	2	tablespoons sake
1	cup pork stock		Pepper
1	garlic clove, crushed or minced	2 to 3	tablespoons cornstarch dissolved in 1/4 cup cold water
1/2	tablespoon brown sugar		

Put the knuckles in a pot of water, bring to a boil, and cook, covered at a low boil until well done. Remove them from the pot and bone them. The meat will come right off if they are well cooked.

In another pot, mix the stock, garlic, sugar, sake, and pepper. Bring to a rapid boil and let it reduce for at least 5 minutes.

Thicken with the cornstarch paste using enough to make the stock semithick. Add the pork, heat through, and serve.
Serves 4

BROILED HAWAIIAN HAM STEAK

	Oil		Sprinkling of cinnamon
1	ham steak	2	pineapple rings
1	tablespoon brown sugar	1	maraschino cherry

*O*il the bottom of a broiling pan. Broil the ham steak on high, browning each side. Remove from the broiler and keep hot. Combine the sugar and cinnamon. Place the pineapple rings in a shallow baking pan and put the cherry in the center. Sprinkle the sugar mixture on top and broil, turning once, until browned on both sides. Place the rings on the ham and spoon the juice from the baking pan on top.
Serves 1

CREAMED HAM ON A CROISSANT

16 to 24	ounces cooked ham		Roux (equal parts flour and butter, cooked)
2	tablespoons butter or 4 tablespoons ham stock	1	package frozen peas
2	cups half-and-half	4	large or 8 small croissants

*C*ut the ham into bite-size pieces. Sauté in a bit of butter or the ham stock until hot. Add the half-and-half, thicken with the roux, and add the peas. Heat through. To serve, cut the croissants in half and ladle on some of the creamed ham.
Serves 4

Lamb

*L*amb is not only very economical but delicious. Prepared properly, it can be a blessing when you are at your wits' end trying to cook something different, wholesome, and pleasing.

First, learn the type of cuts and how to cook them.

The leg can be purchased as a whole. You can have the butcher cut several lamb steaks from it and have an extra dinner in the future.

The chops and T-bones are the smaller rib section. If you are inclined really to put on the dog, have the butcher make a nice crown roast for you.

The shanks are the foreleg. You can bake them in a special marinade and really make a guest's mouth water.

The shoulder is the least expensive cut, but you can stuff it and have a real beauty of a roast.

THE DINGO ROAST LEG OF LAMB

2 garlic cloves, minced
2 tablespoons lemon juice
  Salt
  Pepper
2 bay leaves, finely
  crumbled
  Large pinch of thyme
  Several leaves of fresh
  dill

1 tablespoon wine
  vinegar
1 leg of lamb, about 6 to
  8 pounds
4 whole garlic cloves
2 cups mirepoix (coarsely
  chopped celery,
  carrots, and onions)
  Roux (equal parts flour
  and butter, cooked)

*M*ix the minced garlic, lemon juice, salt, pepper, bay, thyme, dill, and vinegar. Make 4 holes in the leg and insert the whole garlic cloves. Rub the entire leg with the mixture of the seasonings and place the leg in a roasting pan, setting it on the mirepoix. Add a small amount of water. Roast at 425° for 15 minutes, then turn the oven down to 325° and roast the leg to doneness, figuring about 1½ hours for rare, 2½ hours for medium, and so on. (To check for doneness, insert a metal fork into the meaty part of the leg, leave it in for a slow count of five, take it out, and touch your lip with it. If it is cold, the meat is raw; just slightly warm, very rare. The more heat you feel, the more the leg is cooked. It's really that easy.) Add water as needed, and put in enough to make gravy later.

Once the roast is done, remove it and deglaze the pan over a stove burner. Add more water, if needed, and thicken with the roux. Strain this through a sieve or strainer and you have your gravy. Serve it with the roast and you have a beautiful dinner.

Serves 10 to 12

THE HAWAIIAN DECAMBRA LEG ROAST

1	leg of lamb, boned	1/2	cup orange juice
1/4	teaspoon marjoram	1/2	cup pineapple juice
1/4	teaspoon thyme	1	small onion, chopped
1	tablespoon mild prepared mustard	1	jigger Tokay wine
		4	sprigs parsley
1/2	teaspoon each grated orange and lemon zest	2 to 4	tablespoons arrowroot powder (optional)

*R*ub the leg of lamb with the seasonings and herbs. Place in a pan. Add the remaining ingredients, except the arrowroot, to the pan. Roast at 425° for 15 to 20 minutes. Turn the heat down to 325° and finish to the desired doneness. Be certain to baste the lamb frequently. Remove the lamb from the pan and strain the stock. If you wish to thicken the stock, mix arrowroot with a bit of water, heat the stock, and thicken as you like.
  Serves 6

Stafford L. DeCambra is head chef instructor at the University of Hawaii.

LAMB CHOPS DU BARRY

12	small lamb chops	1	package or bunch fresh mint, very finely chopped
	Butter		
4	tablespoons water		
4	tablespoons white wine	4	tablespoons sugar
		4	tablespoons mint jelly
			Applesauce

*Y*ou can broil or charbroil lamb chops, but for this dish I suggest pan-frying in butter. When done, remove. Deglaze the pan with the water and wine. Add the mint. Sauté for a few minutes, then add the sugar and mint jelly over a low flame. When the sauce is done, strain it through a sieve. Serve the sauce all over the chops, with applesauce on the side.

Serves 6

LAMB CHOPS WITH FETA CHEESE, OLIVES, AND TOMATO SAUCE

	Greek olive oil		Salt
6	thick loin lamb chops		Pepper
2	garlic cloves, minced	18	chopped black Greek
1	small onion, minced		olives
	Several pinches of	1	cup chopped peeled
	oregano		tomatoes
1	cup good Greek wine	1/2	pound feta cheese
	(retsina)		

*H*eat the oil and sauté the chops in a pan until just done. Add the garlic and onion and sauté for a few minutes. Do not brown them. Add the oregano, wine, salt, and pepper. Turn the heat down to low and cook the chops until just tender, which should take no more than half an hour. Remove the chops from the pan. Add the olives and tomatoes and cook for a few minutes. Mix in the feta cheese and serve over the chops.

Serves 6

CROWN ROAST OF LAMB WITH SIX VEGETABLES

1	crown roast	16	round potatoes, about
	Olive oil		1 1/2 inches in
	Salt		diameter
	Pepper	1	head cauliflower
16	cherry tomatoes	4	carrots, cut into 1-inch
1	bunch broccoli		rounds
16	medium-sized		Mint sauce (page 255)
	mushrooms		

*R*ub the roast with oil and salt and pepper. Wrap pieces of aluminum foil around the tips of the bones so they will not burn. Cook the roast in a large pan in a 360° oven (15 minutes per pound for a rare roast). On the side, cook all the vegetables. The tomatoes can be blanched for a few minutes. (You can cook them longer if you prefer, but keep in mind that vegetables should not be overcooked.)

Remove the roast from the oven. Take off the foil and replace it with paper panties. Fill the center of the roast with the vegetables, intermixed. Serve with mint sauce.

Serves 8

BRAISED BREAST OF LAMB

1	5- to 6-pound breast of lamb		celery, carrots, and onions)
	Oil	1/2	teaspoon marjoram
	Salt	1/4	cup tomato purée
	Pepper		Lamb stock
2	bay leaves, crumbled		Roux (equal parts flour
1	cup mirepoix (chopped		and butter, cooked)

*R*ub the breast with oil, salt, pepper, and bay leaves. Place it in a pan. In a 425° oven, roast until slightly browned. Add the mirepoix, marjoram, tomato purée, and stock. Cover the pan and turn the oven down to 325°. Braise the roast until it is very tender. Remove the breast and deglaze the pan on top of the stove. Thicken it with the roux and strain the gravy.

Serves 6

ROAST STUFFED LAMB

Bread Stuffing

3   celery stalks
1   large onion
1   garlic clove, minced or
     pressed
4   tablespoons butter
2   cups diced bread or
     unflavored croutons
4   tablespoons Tokay
     Crushed peppercorns to
     taste
1   tablespoon caraway
     seeds
4   pounds boned lamb
     shoulder, all fat
     trimmed off

Oil
1   teaspoon dried
     rosemary
Salt
Pepper
2   cups mirepoix (chopped
     celery, carrots, and
     onions)
1   quart lamb or beef
     stock
     Roux (equal parts flour
     and butter, cooked)

*S*auté the celery, onion, and garlic in the butter. Add to the bread cubes and mix in the Tokay, peppercorns, and caraway seeds.

Stuff the shoulder and tie it with twine. Rub it with the oil, rosemary, salt, and pepper. Roast at 325° for at least 2 hours. Add the mirepoix and the stock. Rotate the lamb and cook for another half hour. Remove the lamb. Thicken the stock with the roux and strain it. To serve, slice the lamb and set it down on the gravy, or serve the gravy on the side.

Serves 6 to 8

O'SHAUGHNESSY'S IRISH STEW

3   pounds cubed lamb
     from the shoulder
3   large carrots, cut into
     bite-size pieces

6   small potatoes, cut in
     half
1   very small turnip
6   pearl onions

2	leeks, white part only, cut up		Butter
1/4	teaspoon marjoram	1	small package frozen mixed vegetables
	Salt		Roux (equal parts flour and butter, cooked)
	Pepper to taste		

*P*ut the meat, carrots, and potatoes in a large pot, cover with water, and bring to a boil. Turn the heat down to a simmer and cook until the meat is tender. Skim off the excess grease with a skimmer and paper towels. Cook the turnip separately. Add it to the pot. Sauté the onions, leeks, marjoram, salt, and pepper in butter. Add to the pot and simmer for about 15 minutes, to incorporate all the flavors. Add the frozen mixed vegetables and let everything simmer for 5 minutes. Strain the contents into another pot, thicken the stock with the roux, and put everything back together.
Serves 6

LAMB FRICASSEE

3	pounds lamb, cut into 1-inch cubes	1/4	cup chopped fresh mint
	Roux (equal parts flour and butter, cooked)		Salt
			Pepper

*C*ook the lamb in 2 quarts water until tender. Skim the top, then strain the stock and thicken it with the roux. Replace the meat. Add the mint and reheat. Season and serve over noodles.
Serves 6

INDIA'S CURRIED LAMB

1	shoulder of lamb (about 4 pounds)	1/2	cup mirepoix (celery, carrots, and onions cut into 1/2-inch dice)
2	quarts lamb stock		
1	small onion, chopped		Butter

1/2 cup flour
2 tablespoons hot curry
   powder
1 teaspoon cumin
1/4 teaspoon powdered
   cloves
1 tablespoon chopped
   fresh fennel or
   teaspoon fennel
   seeds
3 tablespoons grated
   coconut

1 teaspoon grated orange
   zest
1/2 teaspoon grated lemon
   zest
3 tablespoons brown
   sugar
1 large apple, cored and
   cut into small dice
1 banana, puréed

*C*ube the lamb and cook it in the stock. Skim the stock; remove the lamb. In a large pot, sauté the onion and mirepoix in butter. Mix the flour, curry powder, cumin, cloves, fennel, and coconut. Add to the pot and cook slightly. Add the stock slowly and cook for a few minutes. Purée in a food processor or a blender and return to the pot. Add the zests, meat, and sugar. Ten or 15 minutes later, add the apple and cook for a few minutes, then add the bananas. Bake in a covered casserole dish at 360° until the lamb is very tender. Serve over rice.

Serves 6

MARY'S LAMB SHANKS IN SAUCE

4 lamb shanks
   Juice of 1/2 lemon
2 garlic cloves, minced
1 cup flour
1 teaspoon salt
1 teaspoon pepper
1/2 cup mild salad oil
2 cups beef stock

1/2 cup dry vermouth
1/2 cup water
1 large onion, finely
   minced
2 large carrots, cut into
   bite-size pieces
2 celery stalks, cut into
   bite-size pieces

*R*ub the shanks with lemon juice and garlic. Set aside for at least a half hour.

Mix the flour, salt, and pepper and rub the shanks with the mixture. Save the rest of the flour for thickening the sauce.

Brown the shanks in oil. Take them out of the pan; add the remaining flour and cook into a roux for the sauce. Add the beef stock, vermouth, and water. Stir until smooth. (If it does not become smooth, strain it.) Add the onion and cook. Place the shanks and sauce in a baking dish and cook in a 325° oven for 2 hours.

Turn the shanks over and add the carrots and celery to the dish. Put it back in the oven and bake for about another hour, until you can feel the tenderness of the shanks. Serve with buttered noodles on the side.

Serves 4

GREEK LAMB CURRY

2 onions, sliced	1/2 teaspoon curry
3 garlic cloves, chopped	powder, or more to
4 tablespoons melted	taste
butter	1/4 cup flour
Juice of 1 lemon	3 cups cubed cooked
Salt	lamb
Pepper	4 tablespoons Madeira
	11/2 cups chicken stock

*S*auté the onions and garlic in butter in the bottom of a casserole dish. Use the lemon juice to wet the meat. Mix the salt, pepper, and curry powder with the flour, and roll the lamb in it. Take the onion and garlic out of the casserole, add a bit more butter for frying, and lightly brown the lamb. Add the onions and garlic and the remaining ingredients, then cover the dish and bake at 360° for about an hour. The whole thing should be thickened enough from flouring the meat. However, if it is not thick enough, you can thicken it a bit more with a roux (equal parts flour and butter, cooked).

Serves 6

A good way to use leftover lamb.

POULTRY

Chicken and a Turkey

Chickens are likely to be contaminated with salmonella, so wash them well, inside and out, in salted water with a little vinegar.

ROAST CHICKEN

1   6- to 8-pound roaster   Pepper to taste
    Salt   1   small jar mayonnaise

*W*ash the chicken and dry it well. Rub the chicken inside and out with salt, pepper, and mayonnaise. Bake at 375° until crusty brown (which will be accomplished by the mayonnaise on the chicken skin), 10 to 12 minutes per pound. That's it!
  Serves 4 to 6

CHICKEN BREASTS DIPPED IN HONEY WITH CRUSHED ALMONDS (POULETTE ALMONDE DE VIN)

4   boneless, skinless   4   tablespoons butter
    chicken breasts,   2   tablespoons lemon
    flattened   juice
1   pint light honey (not   1/4   cup sauterne
    dark)   1   pint heavy cream
8   ounces almonds,
    chopped and
    crushed

*D*ip the breasts in honey, then coat with almonds. Sauté in butter until done, approximately 4 minutes per side. Remove the breasts and deglaze the pan with lemon juice and sauterne. Add the cream, reduce the heat, and cook until the sauce is as thick as a cream sauce. Serve over the chicken.
  Serves 4

CHICKEN PALOISE

1	2¹/₂-pound chicken, cut into 8 pieces	2	garlic cloves, crushed
	Salt	1	cup sliced mushrooms
	Pepper	1/4	pound cooked ham, diced
4	tablespoons olive oil	1/2	cup dry white wine
3	tomatoes, peeled and chopped	3	tablespoons armagnac or cognac
3	green peppers, seeded and sliced lengthwise		Chopped fresh parsley

*S*eason the chicken pieces with salt and pepper. Heat the olive oil in a heavy casserole or saucepan and sauté the chicken until golden brown, about 10 minutes. Add the tomatoes, green peppers, garlic, mushrooms, ham, and wine. Cover and cook gently for half an hour, or until the chicken is tender. Remove the chicken to a hot platter, blend the sauce with a whisk, and reduce it until fairly thick. Return the chicken to the pan, pour armagnac over it, and ignite. Let the flames die out and sprinkle with parsley.

Serves 8

CHINESE-HAWAIIAN CHICKEN ANISE

8	tablespoons melted chicken fat (see note)	2	tablespoons dark brown sugar
2	3- to 4-pound chickens, disjointed	4	tablespoons soy sauce
8	small scallions, cut into 1-inch lengths	2/3	cup anisette or Pernod
		2	cups chicken stock

*H*eat the fat in a large skillet. Brown the chicken pieces well on all sides and remove from the skillet. Add the scallions to the skillet and sprinkle with sugar and soy sauce. Combine the liqueur and stock, return the chicken to the skillet, and pour the liqueur mixture over it. Cook, uncovered, over low heat for 30 minutes. Turn the heat to high and cook, several pieces of chicken at a time, until the skin is browned and crisp. The liquid will boil off almost entirely. Serve with plain or fried rice, if you wish.

Serves 12

Note: Pick off any pieces of fat from the chickens and melt them in a small frying pan. If there is not enough to make 8 tablespoons, add safflower oil to make up the difference.

CHICKEN WITH MINT AND ORANGE SAUCE

5	mint sprigs plus more for garnish	1/4	cup orange juice
1	3- to 3 1/2-pound chicken	1/2	cup chicken stock
4	tablespoons softened butter	1/2	stick (4 tablespoons) cold butter, cubed
	Salt	2	tablespoons chopped fresh mint
	Pepper	1	teaspoon grated orange zest
2	tablespoons Grand Marnier		Orange slices

*P*ut 5 mint sprigs in the cavity of the chicken and truss to close it up. Rub the skin with softened butter and season with salt and pepper. Place the chicken, breast side up, on a rack in a preheated 450° oven and immediately reduce the heat to 350°. Roast for 1 to 1 1/4 hours, basting every 15 minutes.

Place the chicken on a warm platter and remove the mint sprigs from the cavity. Pour off excess fat from the roasting pan. On top of stove deglaze the pan with the remaining juices and Grand Marnier. Add the orange juice and chicken stock and bring to a boil, stirring to pick up any roasted bits left in the pan. Transfer the liquid to a small heavy saucepan and reduce by half over high heat. You should have about 1/2 cup. Remove from the heat and whisk in the cold butter, a piece at a time. Add the chopped mint and grated zest. Put the chicken on a platter and garnish with orange slices and mint sprigs. Serve the sauce separately.

Serves 4

CHICKEN OR TURKEY TETRAZZINI

1	pound fettuccine noodles or spaghetti	8 to 12	ounces grated Parmesan cheese
	About 2 tablespoons olive oil	8	medium-size mushrooms, thinly sliced
1	small onion, minced		Roux (equal parts flour and butter, cooked) (optional)
2	garlic cloves, minced		
1	quart heavy cream	18 to 24	ounces cooked chicken or turkey meat

Cook the noodles *al dente.* In a large saucepan, heat the olive oil and sauté the onion, then the garlic, until just done. Add the cream, heat, and whip in three fourths of the cheese. In a skillet, sauté the mushrooms in a little oil until completely cooked. If you like, thicken the cheese sauce slightly with the roux. Add the mushrooms. Slice the chicken or turkey meat into strips about 1/4 inch thick and 2 to 3 inches long. Add to the sauce and mix well. Mix the sauce with the noodles, place in individual casserole dishes, and top with the remaining cheese. Bake in a 350° oven only until the top shows a slight browning, then remove and serve.

Serves 6 to 8

Leftovers? There is no such thing. There may be slices or pieces of chicken or turkey left from the original meal, but don't let anyone tell you that these are leftovers and shouldn't be served to honored guests. Here is a dish I would serve my most revered of friends with pride. You should not feel any embarrassment about using things that were part of another meal. If you had to make the dish from scratch, you would have to cook the meat first anyway. See what I mean?

ROAST TURKEY WITH STUFFING

1	10-pound turkey	3	onions, coarsely chopped
	Salt	4	carrots, coarsely chopped
	Pepper	2	cups water
	Poultry seasoning		
1	bunch parsley		
6	celery stalks, coarsely chopped		

*W*ash the turkey and pat dry. Season the cavity with salt, pepper, and poultry seasoning. Put the parsley and half of the celery, onions, and carrots in the cavity. Put the other half in a roasting pan, along with the water. Place the turkey in the pan, cover it with a foil tent, and set it in a 325°oven. Roast for approximately 3 hours. Remove the foil and baste the turkey with the pan juices every 10 minutes until it is golden brown. To check for doneness, insert a fork into the thigh. If the liquid runs clear, the turkey is done. Serve with one of the following stuffings.

Serves 6 to 8

Chestnut Stuffing

1	loaf white bread, crusts trimmed off, cut into cubes	6	celery stalks, cut into 1/2-inch dice
1/2	cup milk	1	can chestnuts, chopped
2	tablespoons rubbed sage	1/2	cup white wine
1	large onion, cut into 1/2-inch dice		Salt
			Pepper
			Melted butter

*S*oak the bread cubes in milk. Combine with the sage, onion, celery, chestnuts, wine, salt, and pepper. Turn it into a buttered baking dish, drizzle with melted butter, and bake in a 350° oven for approximately 1 hour, until the top is browned.

Serves 6 to 8

Ground Beef and Mashed Potato Stuffing

1   pound ground beef,
    cooked and crumbled
    Salt
    Pepper
1   onion, cut into 1/2-inch
    dice

1   tablespoon poultry
    seasoning
3   cups mashed potatoes
    Melted butter

*C*ombine the beef, salt, pepper, onion, poultry seasoning, and mashed potatoes. Turn into a buttered baking dish, drizzle with melted butter, and bake in a 350° oven for approximately 1/2 hour, until browned.
    Serves 6 to 8

Sausage Stuffing

1   box seasoned croutons
1/2   pound ground sausage,
    cooked and
    crumbled
1   tablespoon poultry
    seasoning

1   tablespoon rubbed
    sage
1/2   cup white wine
1   cup diced red and
    green peppers
1   small onion, diced
2   celery stalks, diced

*P*repare as in the previous recipe.
    Serves 6 to 8

Duck and Game Birds

*M*ost of us are quite familiar with turkey, chicken, and even Cornish game hen, but not too many of us have done much with duck, goose, guinea hen, pheasant, grouse, quail, or partridge. The following recipes can be used with any of them.

ROAST WILD DUCK, AMERICAN INDIAN STYLE

1	4- to 5-pound wild duck	1	tablespoon black peppercorns
1	cup plain, uncooked maple sap, or 1/4 cup maple syrup mixed with hot water		Large handful of wild scallions or fresh chives
1	teaspoon sea salt		Husks of 12 ears of corn

*R*ub the duck with the sap, then with the salt. Place the peppercorns and scallions in the cavity of the bird. Wrap the duck with the corn husks and bake in a preheated oven at 325° for 2¹/₂ to 3 hours.

Remove the bird from the oven; strain the juices from the pan and set aside. Place the bird on a racked pan, put it back in the oven, and bake it to a crispy stage. Serve the bird, thinly sliced, with some of the strained juices on it.

Serves 4

ROAST PEKING DUCK

1	4- to 5-pound duck	3	bunches scallions, white part only
4	tablespoons molasses		
2	tablespoons rice wine	4	tablespoons hoisin sauce

*W*ash the duck well, removing all the fat you can. Boil a large pot of water and dip the duck in the boiling water for about 5 minutes. Tie the duck up and hang it in a nice cool, airy spot for half a day. Mix the molasses, rice wine, and a bit of water, rub the duck with the mixture, then hang the duck overnight.

Preheat the oven to 350°. Place the duck on a rack in a roasting pan and roast for 1¹/₂ hours. Raise the temperature to 425° and roast the duck for another 15 to 20 minutes. Take the bird out of the oven, skin it as best you can without ruining any of the meat, reserve the skin, and slice the meat into strips 2 to 3 inches long. Place the meat in the center of a serving platter, brush it with hoisin sauce, and lay the scallions over it. Cut the skin into strips and place around the meat.

Serves 4

PRESSED DUCK

1	4- to 5-pound duck	2	tablespoons anise
1	teaspoon saltpeter		pepper
6	tablespoons salt		

*W*ash the duck and remove all the fat you can, then dry it well. Mix the saltpeter, salt, and anise pepper and rub the duck with it, inside and out. Place the duck on a rack in a pan and refrigerate, covered, for 3 days, then hang it out in the sun for a day.

Cut the duck into quarters and wash away the salt mixture with cold water. Put the duck in a large steamer, place a weight on it, and steam it for at least an hour, turning it once or twice. You can then set it aside until you are ready to use it. It will keep for a week or even more, depending on good refrigeration.

When ready to use, either fry it in sesame oil, safflower oil, or the like, or just lightly sauté it.

Serves 4

DRUNKEN DUCK

1	4- to 5-pound duck	1/4	cup sesame oil
1	tablespoon minced garlic	2	cups beer
3	tablespoons soy sauce	3	tablespoons cornstarch, mixed with water
1/8	cup sugar		
3	tablespoons chopped scallions		

*R*emove the fat from the duck and wash it well, then dry it and cut it into quarters. Mix the garlic, soy sauce, sugar, and scal-

lions and rub the mixture all over the duck. In a large pot, heat the oil, then sauté the duck quarters in it. Take the duck out of the pot; add beer to the pot and bring to a boil. Add the duck, reduce the heat, cover, and simmer for 1 to 1½ hours. When you are sure the duck is done, take it out of the pot, strain the juices, and thicken with the cornstarch paste. Slice the duck into bite-size pieces and serve with the sauce.
Serves 4

SPICY GINGER DUCK

1	5- to 6-pound duck		Cornstarch dissolved
4	tablespoons sesame oil		in cold water
12	slices ginger root	8	tablespoons sake
	Zest of 1 orange, cut into pieces		

*W*ash the duck, pull off all the fat, then dry the duck and cut it into pieces. Heat the oil in a large skillet, add the ginger and orange zest, and sauté the duck until a dark, rich golden brown. Remove the duck; strain the juices and thicken with the cornstarch paste. Strain through cheesecloth, add the sake and cook it down just a bit, then serve it with the duck.
Serves 4

SPICY STUFF-A-DUCK

1	5- to 6-pound duck	3	garlic cloves, finely chopped
2	tablespoons ground coriander	½	cup ground almonds
1	teaspoon ground cumin	3	onions, thinly sliced
¼	teaspoon saffron	½	teaspoon dried red chili peppers
½	teaspoon ground anise	2	teaspoons salt
2	teaspoons ground ginger root	1½	cups plus fresh coconut milk, or ¾ cup coconut cream plus ¾ cup water

2 hard-boiled eggs, chopped	2 cups dried bread cubes
	1/2 cup sake

*R*eserve the duck giblets. Wash and dry the duck, remove all the fat you can, and set aside. Grind the coriander, cumin, saffron, anise, ginger, onions, garlic, and almonds. Mix with the sliced onions, chili peppers, salt, and coconut milk and cook in a saucepan over low heat. Grind the giblets, add the hard-boiled eggs, and add to the cooked stuffing mixture. Toss the bread cubes in the sake, add to the stuffing mixture, and fill the cavity of the bird. (If the stuffing seems too dry, use a little more coconut milk to soften it before stuffing the duck.) Rub the bird with coconut milk and bake it in a roasting pan at 425° for 2 1/2 hours, or until the duck becomes tender and is done.

Serves 4

Variation: Curry Ducky. Omit the almonds, coriander, cumin, and anise, and instead add 1 teaspoon mild curry powder.

FISH AND SHELLFISH

COURT BOUILLON

1	bay leaf	1	cup dry white wine, or 1/4 cup lemon juice, or 1/3 cup vinegar
1	thyme sprig, fresh or dried		
10 to 12	parsley sprigs		
1	small onion, sliced	1	quart water
6	peppercorns	1	small carrot, sliced
		1	teaspoon salt

*T*ie together the bay leaf, thyme, and parsley to make a bouquet garni. Combine all of the ingredients in a nonaluminum saucepan and simmer for 20 to 30 minutes. Strain, and use to poach seafood.

Makes 1 quart

JAPANESE BAKED FISH

4	whole trout, cleaned and gutted	8	pieces candied ginger, sliced
	Juice of 4 lemons	4	teaspoons soy sauce
8	bacon slices, rendered and fat reserved		Large pinch of ground anise seed
16	large leaves Savoy cabbage	4	lemons, sliced
4	large mushrooms, sliced		Cornstarch dissolved in cold water
			Salt
			White pepper

*W*ash the fish, pat dry, and rub with lemon juice. Make shallow incisions at an angle across one side (to be the top) of the fish, such as you see on French breads. Grease a large baking pan with bacon fat, line it with the cabbage leaves, and place the fish on the leaves. Put mushroom and ginger slices in the fish cavities. Sprinkle the fish with soy sauce and anise. Lay slices of lemon on the fish, and bake at 350° for 30 minutes, basting with the pan drippings. Remove the fish from the pan and cover with the cabbage. Strain the liquid from pan and thicken slightly with a bit of cornstarch paste. Season the sauce to taste and serve it on the side.

Serves 4

SAUTÉED BROOK TROUT

4   trout, cleaned and
      gutted
     Butter
2   shallots, chopped
2   garlic cloves
12 small shrimp, peeled
      and deveined
12 small shucked oysters,
      with their liquor

4   jiggers dry or semidry
      sherry
     Juice of 1 lemon
2   large pinches Paul
      Prudhomme's
      Seafood Magic
      Seasoning

*I*n a very large skillet, cook the trout in butter. Set aside. Sauté the shallots, then add the garlic and cook briefly. Add the shrimp, then the oysters and their liquor. Cook for just a few moments, then add the wine, lemon juice, and seafood seasoning. Serve the sauce under the trout on dinner plates.

Serves 4

Note: I have often been asked what I consider the best way to cook fish and why. I have eaten fish prepared in every possible manner and can honestly say that the best piece of fish I ever ate was cooked in an iron skillet in a hobo camp back in the thirties. It was simply sautéed, covered with lemon juice and wine and a bit of onion—and that was it.

BAKED FISH WITH CRAB MEAT STUFFING

1 cup crumbs from day-old bread
2 tablespoons butter
1 rounded tablespoon minced fresh parsley
1/2 teaspoon plus salt
Pepper

1/3 cup crab meat
11/2 tablespoons mixed lemon juice and dry white wine
1 3-pound sheepshead (porgy), cleaned
Flour
Melted butter

*M*oisten the bread crumbs with cold water. Gently squeeze out any excess, but do not mash them into a paste. Melt butter in a small heavy skillet and fry the crumbs over low but moderate heat for 3 to 4 minutes, adding more butter as the butter in the skillet is absorbed. Add the parsley and 1/2 teaspoon salt, toss, and add pepper to taste. Add the crab meat and lemon juice and wine. Fill the fish cavity and sew up the ventral slit or fasten with toothpicks. Dredge the fish in flour seasoned with salt and pepper. Shake off any excess. Place in a buttered baking dish, add water just to cover the bottom of the pan, and bake at 400° for 45 to 50 minutes, allowing 16 minutes per pound. Every 10 to 15 minutes, baste with the pan juices and melted butter.

Serve with boiled potatoes, buttered and sprinkled with chopped parsley. On the side, serve a sauceboat with lemon butter (melted butter with lemon juice added). Brown butter or even anchovy butter may also be served with it.

Serves 4 or 5

POACHED WHOLE SALMON

3 cups dry white wine
3 cups court bouillon (page 92)
3 tablespoons black peppercorns
3 lemons, sliced

2 cups sliced mirepoix (equal parts onion, celery, and carrots)
1 bunch parsley
1 4- to 6-pound salmon, gutted and scaled

*P*ut all of the ingredients, except the salmon, in a poacher with 3-inch-high sides and bring to a boil. Reduce the heat to a simmer, place the salmon over the liquid, and lightly poach until done, approximately 45 minutes. Do not boil it. Serve hot, or let the fish cool in the liquid, then remove to a platter.
    Serves 4

BROILED SWORDFISH WITH LEMON BUTTER

4	swordfish steaks (about 8 ounces each)		Juice of 1 whole lemon
8	tablespoons melted butter (1 stick)	4	tablespoons dry white wine
		8	lemon slices

*B*rush the steaks with melted butter, pour a bit of lemon juice on them, and broil them about 4 inches from the flame of the broiler; turn them once and repeat the process. Mix the wine and remaining butter and lemon juice. When the fish is nearly done, place 2 slices of lemon on each steak and broil to finish. Set the steaks on a large platter, pour on the sauce, and serve.
    Serves 4

SALMON STEAKS WITH DILL BUTTER

8	tablespoons (1 stick) butter, softened	4	tablespoons chopped fresh dill
	Salt	2	tablespoons lemon juice
	Pepper	4	salmon steaks (1½ inches thick)

*C*ombine the butter, salt, pepper, dill, and lemon juice. Place the salmon steaks in a buttered pan and cover with dill butter. Bake in a preheated 375° to 400° oven for 12 to 14 minutes (or broil for 4 to 6 minutes, turning once), until the center bone is easily removed, approximately 12 minutes.
    Serves 4

POACHED SALMON FILLETS WITH McDOLE'S MUSHROOM CREAM SAUCE

4 6-ounce salmon fillets
1 teaspoon finely chopped
      shallots
2 cups dry white wine
2 tablespoons Dijon
      mustard

2 cups sliced mushrooms
1 cup heavy cream
2 tablespoons finely
      chopped fresh parsley

*L*ightly poach the fillets with shallots and wine. Remove the fillets to a warm oven. Add mustard to the pan and reduce until almost dry. Add the mushrooms and cream and reduce to the desired thickness. Add the parsley and pour over the fillets.
Serves 4

SAUTÉED SOLE WITH DILLY SAUCE SUZANNE

4 sole fillets
2 celery stalks, finely
      diced
1 carrot, finely diced
1/4 cup Chablis
1 teaspoon Paul
      Prudhomme's
      Seafood Magic
      Seasoning

2 tablespoons lemon
      juice
1/2 cup heavy cream
4 dill sprigs, finely
      chopped

*S*auté the sole and remove it to a warm holding area. Sauté the celery, carrot, wine, seafood seasoning, and lemon juice. Add the cream and dill, reduce by half, and serve over the fillets.
Serves 4

FRIED FISH FILLETS

2   eggs, lightly beaten
1   cup flour
2   cups dry bread crumbs,
      seasoned with salt
      and pepper

4   fish fillets
      Mixture of oil and
      butter

*W*ash the fish fillets and pat dry. Powder them with flour and dip in egg wash, then bread crumbs. Heat a skillet, add the mixture of oil and butter, and sauté the fish fillets until golden brown. Serve with lemon wedges and/or tartar sauce.
Serves 4

Variation: Use the beer batter on page 6.

LOBSTER SAVANNAH

2   large lobsters (2 to 3
      pounds each)
2   cups plus Newburg
      sauce (page 243)
4   very large shrimp
4   very large oysters

     Meat from 4 Alaskan
       king crab meat legs
1   cup crab meat stuffing
       (page 10; see note
       below)
1   cup hollandaise sauce
       (page 245)

*C*ook the lobsters until they turn red. Cut them open from the top, remove the stomachs and intestinal veins and discard. Remove the meat from the tails and claws. Heat the Newburg sauce, add the shrimp, cook slightly, add the oysters, cook slightly, then add the crab meat and lobster meat. Do not let the sauce come to a boil at any time, and be certain that it is very thick, so it will not run out of the lobster shells. Fill the lobster cavities with the sauced meat, then top with crab meat dressing. Place in a 375° oven and heat until the inside is hot. Remove from the oven and pour hollandaise sauce over the crab meat dressing. Set under a broiler until it becomes a light golden color and bubbly. Place each lobster on a large platter and serve. Each is meant to serve two people.

Serves 4
Note: Make the crab meat stuffing using less butter than called for; it should be on the dry side.

CRAB FARCI

2   cups crab meat
1   stick (8 tablespoons) plus butter
1/4 cup slivered scallions, with part of the green
1/2 cup soft white bread crumbs
    Juice of 1/2 lemon, strained

2   hard-boiled eggs
    Salt
    Cayenne pepper
1   rounded tablespoon minced fresh parsley
    Fine dry bread crumbs
    Lemon wedges

*P*ick over the crab meat carefully and set aside. Melt the cup of butter in a skillet and sauté the scallions for 2 minutes over moderate heat. Add the crab meat and cook for 2 minutes. Add the soft bread crumbs and toss lightly; cook for 2 to 3 minutes, stirring constantly. Remove from the heat. Mix the lemon juice with enough cold water to make 3 tablespoons and dribble over the crab meat mixture. Toss again. Sieve in the hard-cooked egg yolks and toss. Finely chop the egg whites and toss them with the mixture. Add salt and cayenne to taste and the minced parsley. Toss once more. Pile it into buttered crab shells or ramekins and top with fine dry crumbs. Dot with additional butter and bake at 350° until brown, about 20 minutes. Serve with lemon wedges.
Serves 6 to 8

Variation: In New Orleans the soft bread crumbs were first moistened with cold milk, then gently squeezed dry, combined with sautéed chopped onion and garlic, and seasoned with bay leaf, thyme, and parsley. When this mixture was added to the crab meat, it gave the finished dish a moister, almost sauced consistency.

FROG LEGS CREOLE

14	pairs large frog legs	Fine dry bread crumbs
	Juice of 1/2 lemon	Deep fat for frying
	Salt	Onion cream sauce
	Pepper	(page 244)
2	eggs, well beaten	

*S*cald the frog legs in a large pot of boiling water with the lemon juice, salt, and pepper. Drain them and pat dry. Dip the legs in egg wash and then in bread crumbs. Fry them in deep fat at 375° for 2 to 3 minutes, or until tender. Serve on a bed of onion cream sauce.

Serves 7

CRAWGATOR STEW

2	sticks (1 cup) butter	2	pounds alligator
1	cup flour		meat, cut into
2	quarts chicken		bite-size pieces
	stock	1/2	cup chopped celery
1/2	cup chopped	3	cups diced potatoes
	onions		Several large
3 to 4	tablespoons olive		pinches of Paul
	oil		Prudhomme's
4	garlic cloves		Seafood Magic
1	6-ounce can tomato		Seasoning
	paste	1/2	cup chopped fresh
1	1-pound can		parsley
	tomatoes	2	pounds fresh
			crawfish

*I*n a very large pot, melt the butter and cook the flour slowly in it for a dark brown roux (you must cook it slowly, stirring often in order not to burn it). Slowly add the chicken stock, which will thicken from the roux. In another pot, sauté the onions in olive oil until translucent. Add the garlic, brown it slightly, and discard it. Add the tomato paste and an equal amount of water. Bring to a boil and simmer for 10 minutes.

Add the can of tomatoes and their juice. Cook for a short time, then add the alligator meat. Cook for at least 1 hour.

Add the celery and potatoes. Cook until just done, then add the seafood seasoning and parsley. Turn off the heat and let it marinate overnight in the refrigerator.

Reheat the contents, add the crawfish, cook through and turn the heat off again for another hour or so. Reheat and serve.
Serves 6

This recipe was a gift from my students at Delgado Community College in New Orleans at their graduation buffet. It is original—real Cajun-Creole—and typical of that great city's authentic style of cooking.

DUNBAR'S JAMBALAYA

3	tablespoons butter	1	6-ounce can tomato paste
1	small onion, minced		
1	garlic clove	4	parsley sprigs, minced
1½	pounds shrimp, peeled and deveined	2	thyme sprigs, minced
		2	cups hot water
3	small pork sausages or Cajun andouille		Salt
			Pepper
¼	pound cooked ham	⅓	cup raw rice
1	tablespoon flour		

*M*elt 1 tablespoon butter and brown the onion and garlic. If the shrimp are very large, cut them in half lengthwise. Add the shrimp and cook, stirring, for about 5 minutes, until they are bright pink. Cut the sausages into small pieces and brown in another pan. Cut the ham into cubes the same size as the sausages and sauté with the sausages for a few minutes. Blend in the flour. Combine the meat with the shrimp and add the tomato paste, parsley, and thyme. Add the hot water and bring to a boil. Add salt and pepper to taste, cover, and simmer for 1 hour. Cook the rice according to the directions on the package until it is barely tender. Stir it into the meat mixture and add the remaining butter. Set the pan in a larger pan of hot water and continue to cook for about 30 minutes, or until the rice has absorbed all the liquid and the mixture is quite dry.

Serves 6

OYSTER AND SHRIMP JAMBALAYA

2 tablespoons olive oil
1 pint shucked oysters
2 onions, chopped
1 garlic clove, pressed
1 small green pepper, seeded and minced
1 pound shrimp, peeled and deveined
1 cup raw rice
2 cups (one 1-pound can) tomatoes
2 cups chicken bouillon or water
1 bay leaf
Pinch of ground thyme
1 teaspoon salt
1/8 teaspoon pepper
1 teaspoon sugar
Minced fresh parsley

*H*eat the olive oil in a large skillet. Add the oysters and cook over low heat until the edges begin to curl. Remove them from the pan and refrigerate. Cook the onions, garlic, and green pepper in the skillet for 2 to 3 minutes. Add the shrimp and cook until they turn pink; remove them from the pan. Put the rice in the skillet and cook, stirring constantly, until it turns brown. Add the tomatoes, bouillon, and seasonings. Cover and simmer over low heat until the rice is tender and the liquid has been absorbed. Add the oysters and shrimp, heat through, stirring gently, and serve garnished with parsley.

Serves 6

SALMON CAKES

1 egg, beaten
1/2 cup heavy cream
Salt
Pepper
1 tablespoon chopped fresh dill
2 tablespoons finely minced onion
1 tablespoon lemon juice

1 pound cooked salmon,
boned and crumbled

2 tablespoons crushed
club crackers
Oil

Combine the egg, cream, salt, pepper, dill, onion, and lemon juice. Add the salmon and cracker crumbs. Form into patties and fry in oil until browned and heated through, approximately 4 minutes on each side.

Serves 4

CASSEROLES

So much can be said for casseroles because of their versatility. They can be prepared a great deal ahead of time, frozen, and served at your convenience. Make them as you like, with anything you like.

VEAL-ARTICHOKE DELICIOSO

1/2	cup flour mixed with salt and pepper to taste	7 or 8	pearl onions
2	pounds stew veal, cut into bite-size pieces	3	shallots, finely chopped
		2	pinches marjoram
4	tablespoons olive oil	1	cup veal or chicken stock
4	tablespoons butter	2	pinches of thyme
2	cups finely chopped tomatoes	1	14-ounce can artichoke hearts
		2	hard-boiled eggs, sliced

*F*lour the meat. In a casserole large enough to hold all of the ingredients, brown the meat in a mixture of oil and butter. Add all of the remaining ingredients, except the artichokes and eggs, cover the casserole, and bake at 325° for 15 minutes. Stir in the artichokes and cook, covered, for another 15 minutes. Remove from the oven and garnish with egg slices.

Serves 4

OYSTER AND ARTICHOKE CASSEROLE

40	shucked oysters	12	artichoke hearts, quartered
2	cups oyster liquor		Salt
2	bay leaves		Pepper
1/4	teaspoon thyme	4	teaspoons butter
4	tablespoons roux (flour and butter, cooked)	1/2	cup bread crumbs
2	cups coarsely chopped scallions	1/2	cup grated Parmesan cheese

*I*n a skillet, poach the oysters in the oyster liquor, bay leaves, and thyme until the edges start to curl. Remove them to ramekins. Reduce the oyster liquor to about 1½ cups, add the roux, and blend thoroughly. Add the scallions, artichokes, salt, and pepper. Cook over low heat for about 1 minute. Remove from the heat and add the butter. Spoon the sauce over the oysters. Mix the bread crumbs and Parmesan and sprinkle over the sauce. Bake in a preheated 350° oven for about 10 minutes, until the top is golden brown. Serve immediately, with French bread.

Serves 4

CIOPPINO

1	large onion, finely chopped		Seafood Magic Seasoning
	Butter	2	pinches of oregano
2	garlic cloves, minced		Pinch of dry mustard
2	cups fish stock		Salt
1	1-pound 10-ounce can crushed tomatoes		White pepper
		½	pound each shrimp, scallops, oysters, king crab meat, and haddock
2	celery stalks, finely chopped		
2	carrots, finely grated		
2	pinches of Paul Prudhomme's	4	ounces Romano cheese, grated

*I*n a casserole, sauté the onions in butter until golden brown. Add the garlic and do the same. Add the fish stock, tomatoes, celery, carrots, and all of the seasonings. Simmer for about 1 hour. Add the scallops and cook for 2 minutes. Add the shrimp and cook for another 2 minutes. Add the oysters and cook for yet another 2 minutes. Add the crab meat, turn off the heat, and let sit. Cut the haddock into bite-size pieces, sauté in butter in another pan, then add to the casserole. Sprinkle on the cheese and bake, uncovered, until the cheese takes on a very light golden brown color.

Serves 6

AMERICAN INDIAN VEGETABLE CASSEROLE

4 scallions, finely chopped	3 tomatoes, diced
1 garlic clove, minced	1 red pepper, seeded and sliced
1/4 cup salad oil	1 green pepper, seeded and sliced
1 zucchini, sliced	
1 yellow squash, sliced	1 teaspoon salt
1 eggplant, sliced	1/8 teaspoon each pepper, oregano, cumin, and coriander seed
1 cucumber, seeded and sliced	

*I*n a large saucepan, sauté the scallions and garlic in oil until lightly browned. Mix with all of the remaining ingredients, place in a large casserole dish, cover, and bake at 360° for at least 1/2 hour. Remove the cover, turn the heat down to 325°, and let sit for 15 minutes. Check for doneness.

Serves 6

PORK CHOP CASSEROLE

2 tablespoons olive oil	1 apple, cored and sliced
2 tablespoons butter	2 tablespoons flour
2 small onions	1 pint pork stock
8 pork chops	1/2 cup apple cider
1/2 small can button mushrooms	1/2 tablespoon thyme
	Salt
1 celery stalk, cut into 1-inch pieces	Pepper
	2 tablespoons currant jelly
1 1-pound can tomatoes, chopped	

*H*eat the oil and butter in a very large casserole. Chop the onions and sauté them in the mixture until golden brown. Fry the pork chops in this until browned on both sides. Mix in the rest of the vegetables and the apple and cook. Stir in the flour and cook for 4 to 5 minutes. Add the stock, cider, and thyme, and season to your taste. Add the currant jelly and stir well. Cover and bake at 325° for 1 hour.

Serves 4

PORK, POTATOES, AND SAUERKRAUT

4	large pork cutlets or 8 chops		Large dash of powdered coriander seeds
8	potatoes, unpeeled		Salt
1	1-pound 10-ounce can sauerkraut		Pepper
2	teaspoons caraway seeds	2	tablespoons vodka
			Butter

*C*ook the pork and set aside. Slice the potatoes and cook them until almost done. Season the sauerkraut with the caraway seeds, coriander seeds, salt, pepper, and vodka. Butter the bottom of a casserole dish. Put a layer of potatoes on the bottom and top it with the pork, sauerkraut, and another layer of potatoes. Dot the top with butter. Bake at 375° for as long as it takes for the top and bottom layers to cook through. Test with a toothpick or fork to see if the potatoes are soft.

Serves 4

LAMB CASSEROLE

3	large potatoes, thinly sliced	1/2	cup Italian-flavored bread crumbs
2	large zucchini, thinly sliced	1/2	cup grated Romano cheese
1	onion, finely chopped Butter	3	cups diced cooked lamb
3	eggs	2	large tomatoes

*C*ook the potatoes and zucchini. Sauté the onion in a bit of butter. Set aside. Beat the eggs until foamy. Mix the bread crumbs and Romano cheese. Butter a large casserole dish. Place a layer of potatoes on the bottom. Sprinkle a bit bread crumb

mixture on it, and top with some of the lamb, then tomatoes, then zucchini. Pour half the beaten eggs over this. Repeat the process again. Top the whole thing with bread crumb mixture and bake, covered, in a preheated 360° oven for 15 minutes. Remove the cover and bake until the top turns slightly brown.
  Serves 6

If you have lamb left over from a previous meal, try this.

BAKED MACARONI, SAUSAGE, CHEESE, AND TOMATOES

1 pound breakfast-type link sausage	1 pound macaroni
1 pound plus 6 slices American or cheddar cheese	1 1-pound 12-ounce can tomatoes
	Salt
	Pepper

Cook the sausage and save the drippings. Chop the pound of cheese. Cook the macaroni until *al dente* and drain. In a large mixing bowl, mix the sausage drippings with the tomatoes, chopped cheese, and hot macaroni. Season with salt and pepper. Pour into a 3- to 4-quart casserole with a cover. Mix in the sausage, either whole or cut into bite-size pieces. Pour it all into the casserole dish, top with the 6 slices of cheese, and bake, covered, in a preheated 350° oven for about 15 minutes. Uncover and let it sit in the oven just until the cheese is a nice golden brown.
  Serves 4

CAJUN ANDOUILLE, RED BEANS, AND RICE

2 ham hocks	2 cups chopped celery
1 pound dried red kidney beans	1 cup chopped green peppers

1/2 teaspoon garlic
    powder
1   teaspoon Cajun
    seasoning
1   teaspoon Tabasco
    sauce
1   cup finely chopped
    onions

2   bay leaves
1   teaspoon oregano
1/2 teaspoon pepper
1   pound andouille
    sausage
4   cups hot cooked rice

*C*ook the ham hocks in water to make stock; remove the hocks and reserve. Cook the beans, with the next nine ingredients, in the stock. Stir the pot often so the beans will not stick. Halfway through the cooking, add the sausage. The dish is done when the beans are very soft and falling apart. Place the rice in the center of a platter, surround it with the bean mixture, and put the ham hocks at one end and sausage at the other.
    Serves 6

KNACKWURST, SAUERKRAUT, AND POTATO CASSEROLE

1   2-pound package
    sauerkraut, drained,
    juice reserved
1   cup flat beer
2   tablespoons caraway
    seeds
1   large onion, chopped

    Butter
1   large apple
4   links knackwurst (or
    bratwurst)
    Pepper
6   potatoes, peeled and
    thinly sliced

*H*eat the sauerkraut in the beer; drain and season with caraway seeds. Sauté the onion in butter and add it to the sauerkraut. Core and chop the apple and set aside. Heat the sausage in the sauerkraut juice and pepper. Place a layer of half the potatoes in the bottom of a casserole dish, put the sausage on it, top with the sauerkraut, and sprinkle the chopped apple on that. Top with another layer of potatoes. Pour the sauerkraut juice over all and bake, covered, at 350° until you see a great deal of bubbling in the casserole dish. Check the potatoes for doneness with a toothpick, and if they are done, leave the cover off and bake until they reach a nice rich golden brown.

Serves 4

KIELBASA, PULATSKIS, AND CABBAGE CASSEROLE

1	large link kielbasa (Polish sausage)		Salt
			Pepper
1/2	large head cabbage	2	potatoes
4	slices bacon	1/2	large onion, chopped
1	tablespoon caraway seeds	1	egg
		1/4	cup plus flour

Cook the kielbasa till just slightly crisp. Chop the cabbage into bite-size pieces. Chop the bacon the same way. Fry the bacon to crispness. Remove from the pan, reserve, and sauté the cabbage in the bacon fat. Season with caraway seeds and salt and pepper. Return the bacon to the pan.

To make the pulatskis (potato pancakes), peel and slice the potatoes; put them in a food processor, add the onion, egg, and flour, and blend together. If the mixture is too thin, add flour; if too thick, add a bit of milk. Shape into 3 pancakes, each the size of the casserole dish. In a skillet, cook the pancakes till just slightly browned on both sides.

Cut the sausage into lengthwise slices. Put a pancake on the bottom of the casserole dish, then a layer of sausage and a layer of cabbage; top with another pancake and repeat the process. Cover the casserole dish and bake at 350° for 10 minutes. Take the cover off and just slightly dry the top, then serve.

Serves 4

CANADIAN BOUDOIN SAUSAGE CASSEROLE

1	large boudoin (blood sausage)		Salt
6	large potatoes		Pepper
	Butter	1	small onion, finely minced
	Milk	4	large carrots

*C*ook the boudoin until the skin just begins to crack. Set aside. Peel, cut up, and cook the potatoes. Mash them with butter, milk, salt, and pepper, and whip in the onion. Peel the carrots and cut them into uniform lengthwise slices. Cook them until just done.

Butter the bottom and sides of a large casserole dish. Place a layer of mashed potatoes on the bottom. Place a layer of the sausage on this, and a layer of the carrots on that. Top with the remainder of the sausage and another layer of mashed potatoes, and dot the top with bits of butter. Bake, covered, in a preheated 350° oven for 20 minutes. Uncover, brown slightly, and serve.

Serves 4

VEGETABLES

*V*egetables are the real mainstay in our food chain. Without them we would never be able to keep ourselves well. There's no getting away from it.

Vegetables should be eaten raw as often as possible. If you must cook them, do it rapidly, in as short a time as possible. The longer you cook, the less you will garner in the way of nutriments. The Chinese method of cooking is still the best when it comes to retaining most of the vegetables' goodness; they do not cook their vegetables to death. A large skillet is no different from a wok, and in it you can sauté as well as any Chinese chef.

GREEN BEANS AND CHEESE

4	cups cooked green beans	1 1/2	cups grated cheese
1/4	teaspoon salt	2	tablespoons butter
1/8	teaspoon pepper	1/3	cup heavy cream

*P*ut the beans in a buttered baking dish and season with salt and pepper. Add 1/2 cup of the cheese, 1 tablespoon butter, and the cream. Stir until mixed. Sprinkle on with the remaining cheese and dot with the remaining butter. Bake in a preheated 325° oven for about 20 minutes.
Serves 4

BAKED LIMA BEANS

5	tablespoons plus butter	1/2	teaspoon salt
3	tablespoons flour	1/8	teaspoon pepper
1 1/4	cups milk	2	eggs, well beaten
3 1/2	cups cooked lima beans	1/2	cup bread crumbs

*M*elt the 5 tablespoons butter, blend in the flour, add the milk, stir, and cook until thickened. Press the beans through a sieve and combine with the sauce. Add the salt, pepper, and eggs. Pour into a buttered baking dish, cover with the bread crumbs, dot with butter, and bake in a preheated 375° oven for about 20 minutes.
Serves 4

RED BEANS AND RICE

1/2 pound lean salt pork, diced	3 cups cooked rice
1 garlic clove, minced	Minced fresh parsley
2 1/2 cups (1 1-pound 5-ounce can) red kidney beans, drained	Salt Pepper

*F*ry the salt pork until crisp and brown. Remove the pork and reserve; pour off half the fat. Add the garlic to the skillet and cook for 2 to 3 minutes. Add the beans, rice, parsley, and salt and pepper to taste. Heat through. Serve topped with salt pork.
Serves 4

CREOLE WAX BEANS

1/4 cup chopped onions	1 1/2 cups tomato juice
1/4 cup diced green pepper	1/4 teaspoon salt
3 tablespoons butter	1/8 teaspoon pepper
1 1/2 tablespoons flour	3 cups cooked wax beans

*C*ook the onions and green pepper in the butter until the onions are yellow. Blend in the flour, add the tomato juice, and simmer for 5 minutes. Add the salt, pepper, and beans and heat through. Serve hot.
Serves 4

ROSEBUD BEETS AND PINEAPPLE

3/4 cup sugar	1 cup pineapple chunks
2 tablespoons cornstarch	Salt
1/3 cup vinegar	Pepper
1/3 cup water	3 tablespoons butter
4 cups cooked whole small beets	

*C*ombine the sugar and cornstarch; add the vinegar and water. Cook over low heat until thickened and clear; do not boil hard. Add the beets and simmer for 5 minutes. Add the pineapple and heat well. Add the salt, pepper, and butter, heat, and serve.
Serves 4

LADY CABBAGE

1	medium head new cabbage	3	tablespoons butter
1¹/₂	teaspoons salt	¹/₈	teaspoon pepper

*B*ring 1 quart water to a boil in a 3-quart saucepan. Put the cabbage and salt in the boiling water. Bring the water back to a boil and cook the cabbage for 2 minutes. Turn off the heat and let the cabbage stand in the water until tender and light green. Drain the cabbage and add the butter and pepper. Serve hot.
Serves 4

Variation: Chop the cabbage and cook it in bacon fat. Add 1 tablespoon caraway seeds and 6 slices of bacon, cooked and crumbled.

CARROT MOLD

2	cups mashed cooked carrots	¹/₂	cup heavy cream
	Sugar	¹/₂	teaspoon salt
2	eggs, well beaten	¹/₄	teaspoon white pepper
		1	pinch of nutmeg

*S*crape the carrots and slice or halve them. Cook in lightly sweetened water, about 1 tablespoon sugar per quart of water, until tender. Drain and mash them. Measure out 4 cups. Combine the carrots and eggs and then beat with the cream and seasonings. Turn into a buttered ring mold, set the mold in a pan of hot water, and bake in a preheated 375° oven for 30 minutes, or until set. Unmold on a heated serving dish. If you wish, fill the center with some other vegetable; peas, lima beans, or the like would do fine.

Serves 12

Carrots, which came into favor in the early eighteenth century, were nothing to speak of as a general rule save for their flavor when added to soups or stews. You could find them in Indian cooking in this country, for they were much used by them, but the Cajuns did get around to using them in many ways soon after they came here, and eventually carrots became very popular. This dish is from the early eighteenth century.

CAULIFLOWER POLONAISE

1	large head cauliflower		Juice of 1 lemon
8	tablespoons (1 stick) butter	1/4	cup dry sauterne
1/4	pound grated Romano cheese		Salt
			Pepper
1/2	cup seasoned bread crumbs		Paprika

*B*lanch the cauliflower and cut up into small florets. Melt the butter in a skillet and sauté them. As soon as they begin to color slightly, add the cheese, bread crumbs, lemon juice, and wine. Stir with a wooden spoon and turn the florets over and over until they begin to become coated with the ingredients. Season to taste.

Serves 6

CORN PO

3 cups mashed potatoes (see note)	1/2 cup milk or half-and-half
3 tablespoons melted butter	1 cup whole-kernel corn, drained
Salt	Vegetable oil
Pepper	Maple syrup

Combine the potatoes, melted butter, salt, pepper, milk, and corn. Form pancake-size patties and fry in oil until golden brown. Serve with maple syrup.

Serves 4

Note: If you are using leftover mashed potatoes, do not add butter, milk, salt, or pepper.

FRENCH-STYLE PEAS

3 tablespoons butter	2 cups green peas
1/4 cup lean salt pork, diced and blanched	1 teaspoon sugar
1 head romaine lettuce, shredded	2 parsley sprigs
1 medium onion, finely diced	1/4 cup chicken stock
	Large pinch of thyme
	Salt
	Pepper

Heat the butter in a saucepan, add the salt pork, and sauté, stirring often, for 10 minutes. Add the lettuce and sauté for another 5 minutes. Add the remaining ingredients, cover the pan, and simmer for 5 minutes. Uncover and cook until all the liquid has evaporated and the onions and peas are just done.

Serves 6

CREOLE BLACK-EYED PEAS

1/2	pound dried black-eyed peas		Butter
1	dried hot red pepper		Salt
1/4	cup mixed chopped red and green peppers		Pepper
		1/2	small onion, sliced into rings

*I*n a pot, cover the peas with 3 cups cold water. Bring to a boil and boil for 2 minutes. Set aside and let stand for at least 1 hour. Add the dried pepper, bring to a boil, and simmer, covered, for 30 minutes, or until the peas are tender, adding more water if necessary. Stir in the chopped peppers and cook for a few minutes. Season to taste with butter, salt, and pepper. Sauté the onion rings slightly in butter, then serve them on top as a garnish.
Serves 6

BAKED STUFFED POTATOES

2	Idaho baking potatoes	1/4	cup milk or half-and-half
4	tablespoons butter		
1/4	pound cheddar cheese, grated	1/4	pound bacon, cooked and crumbled
	Salt		Melted butter
	Pepper		

*B*ake the potatoes in a 400° oven until firm but done. Let cool. Slice the potatoes in half lengthwise, or cut off the top third. Scoop out almost all of the pulp in both parts. Combine it with the butter, cheese, salt, pepper, and milk. Mash. Mix in the bacon and stuff the potato skins. Drizzle with melted butter and bake at 375° until golden brown.
Serves 4

Variations: Omit the bacon and add half a Spanish onion, diced and sautéed, and 1/2 tablespoon paprika; or 1/4 pound diced cooked chicken; or 1/4 pound cooked sausage meat.

SPANISH FRIES

Oil
1 green pepper, seeded and sliced
1 red pepper, seeded and sliced
1 medium onion, sliced

4 large potatoes, peeled, cubed, and blanched
1 tablespoon capers
6 green olives, sliced
6 black olives, sliced
Salt
Pepper

*H*eat oil in a skillet. Sauté the green and red peppers and onion for 2 minutes. Add the potatoes and sauté until they are golden brown. Add the capers, olives, salt, and pepper. Toss and serve.

Serves 4

JEWISH POTATO KNISHES

Filling

2 medium potatoes
2 tablespoons oil
1 small onion, finely chopped

1/2 teaspoon salt
1/4 teaspoon pepper
1 small egg

Dough

1 cup sifted flour
1/4 teaspoon salt
1/2 teaspoon baking powder

1 egg
1/4 cup oil
1 1/2 tablespoons ice water

*S*crub the potatoes. Put in a pot with water to cover, bring to a boil, then turn the heat down to medium, cover, and cook until soft, about 30 minutes. Pour off the cooking water and pour cold water over the potatoes to cool them. Peel and mash. Heat the oil in a skillet and cook the onion over medium heat until golden brown. Add to the mashed potatoes, along with the salt, pepper, and egg. Mix well and set aside. Put the flour, salt, and baking powder in a bowl. Mix well with a spoon, about 35 to 40 strokes. Add the egg, oil, and ice water. Mix until the dough holds together in a ball. Place the dough on a pastry board and knead until smooth.

Heat the oven to 350°. Butter a cookie sheet.

Divide the dough in half. Dust a rolling pin and half the dough with flour to keep it from sticking. Roll out the dough to a very thin, wide rectangle, about 8 × 12 inches. Brush a few drops of oil on it. Place a strip of the filling, about 1 inch thick, at the top edge of the dough. Roll it up like a jelly roll. Cut the roll into pieces about 2 inches long and put them on the cookie sheet. Repeat with the second piece of dough. Bake for 30 to 35 minutes, until golden brown. Serve the knishes hot, with sour cream. If you must make them ahead of time, reheat them in the oven for about 5 minutes.

Makes 16 to 18

STUFFED SQUASH

3	summer squash	1	thyme sprig
2	ounces lean cooked ham	1	tablespoon chopped fresh parsley
4	ounces cooked and peeled shrimp	1/2	garlic clove, chopped
			Salt
1	onion, sliced		Pepper
1/3	cup butter		Pimiento strips
1/2	cup plus stale French bread crumbs		Parsley sprigs

*W*ash the squash and cook them in boiling salted water to cover until they are tender enough to be pierced with a skewer. Cut the squash in half and scoop out the pulp, being careful not to break the shells. Reserve the shells. Mash the pulp and put it through a food chopper with the ham, shrimp, and onion. Melt 4 tablespoons butter in a heavy skillet and add the ham mixture. Cook over low heat, stirring occasionally, for 20 minutes. Soak the 1/2 cup bread crumbs in water and press them dry.

Add the crumbs to the skillet, along with the thyme, parsley, and garlic. Season with salt and pepper and toss well to blend. Simmer over low heat for 10 minutes, stirring constantly. Pile the stuffing into the squash shells, mounding it high. Sprinkle with more bread crumbs and dot with the remaining butter. Bake in a preheated 350° oven for about 25 minutes, until the topping is golden brown. Garnish each with a strip of pimiento and a parsley sprig. Serve as a side dish.

Serves 6

This is a Japanese favorite I learned in Kyoto. I even served it to the head of the Sumitomo Corp., in 1985 at the Delta Point River Restaurant.

STUFFED ZUCCHINI

	Large pinch of ground ginger		Salt
			Pepper
1	teaspoon soy sauce	1/2	large onion, finely chopped
1	slice bread		
8	ounces mixed leftover meat (beef, veal, bacon, etc.)	3	medium-size zucchini
		1/2	cup canned tomato sauce

Make a stuffing out of all of the ingredients, except the zucchini and tomato sauce. Slice the zucchini in half lengthwise and remove the core. Fill the cavities of the zucchini with stuffing. Lightly butter a baking pan, put the zucchini in it, and bake at 350° for 30 minutes or so, depending on the firmness of the vegetable. Serve with a small amount of tomato sauce on top.

Serves 6

PASTA

*T*he word *pasta* seems to indicate so much that many people become a bit confused by it. The word means "paste," and refers to noodles of various kinds—for example, spaghetti, spaghettini, elbow macaroni, riccolini, amorini, vermicelli, lumache, and lasagna.

The first lesson in pasta is to learn how to cook it properly. Use a great deal of salted water and keep it boiling during the entire cooking process. Never overcook it, for that will indeed turn it to paste; always try to cook it *al dente*, which means cooked yet still firm. Of course, if you are going to recook pasta, as in an oven-baked dish, then you do not cook it nearly as much in the beginning.

RAVIOLI

Dough

4   cups sifted flour
2   teaspoons salt
3   eggs, slightly beaten

Up to 1/4 cup ice
    water
Flour for rolling out

Spinach Filling

Olive oil
1   package frozen spinach,
    thawed and well
    drained
Pepper

2   tablespoons chopped
    fresh parsley
2   hard-boiled eggs, grated
4   ounces mozzarella
    cheese

Sift the flour and salt into a mound on a board or counter top. Make a well in the center and put the eggs in the well. Mix together with one hand, adding ice water, a bit at a time, with the other. Add only enough water to make the dough firm. Flour the board and knead the dough until smooth and elastic. Cut into 4 parts. Roll out each until about 1/8 inch thick, or slightly thinner, if you like. Roll each section loosely in floured towels so it does not dry out while you make the filling.

To make the filling, heat the oil in a skillet. Add the spinach, pepper, and parsley. Heat through, remove from the heat, and add the eggs and cheese. Mix together.

Lay out the first sheet of dough and score it into 1 1/2- to 2-inch squares. If you like, paint the score lines with water, egg wash, or milk, using a pastry brush. Put some filling in the center of each square, then top with another sheet of dough. With a knife, slice through the two layers of dough to cut into squares with the filling inside. Press the edges of the squares together or pinch them all down with a fork, to seal them. Repeat with the remaining dough and filling. Boil the ravioli and serve with a sauce.

Serves 4

Variations: Substitute ricotta or cottage cheese in place of the mozzarella. You can also use cooked meat instead of the cheese, and add just a bit of bread crumbs to bind. Or use one of the stuffings for pasta shells.

This dough and the egg noodles that follow can be cut into many types of pasta—lasagna, fettuccine, spaghettini, cannelloni, etc.

EGG NOODLES

4 cups sifted flour	4 eggs
1 teaspoon salt	1 teaspoon vegetable oil

Sift the flour and salt onto a board or counter top. Make a well in the center. Put the eggs and oil in the well and work it with your fingers until a fine dough is formed. Knead for at least 10 to 15 minutes, until very smooth and elastic. Place in a bowl and set to rest for 20 minutes or so. Divide the dough into 3 parts. Roll out and cut into strips for lasagna or other pasta. Cook *al dente.*
Serves 4

POTATO GNOCCHI

2 pounds potatoes	About 1 1/2 cups flour
2 egg yolks, beaten	1 to 2 tablespoons melted butter
1 1/2 teaspoons salt	

Cook the potatoes. Let cool, peel them, and dry in a pan on the stove, over low heat. Mash. Mix in the yolks, salt, and enough flour to make dough. Mix in melted butter. Roll out to the thickness of a finger. Cut into small pieces and roll them with your fingers into pieces resembling conch shells. Cook for about 10 minutes. Serve with butter and cheese or with a sauce.
Serves 4

THE STANDARD SPAGHETTI SAUCE

1/2	onion, finely minced	2	1-lb 14-ounce cans regular or plum tomatoes, crushed or chopped
	Olive oil		
2	garlic cloves, finely minced		
1	12-ounce can tomato paste	1	large pinch of Italian seasoning
		1	tablespoon sugar
			Pepper
		2	jiggers brandy

Sauté the onion in a bit of oil in a large pot. When just done, add the garlic and sauté until lightly golden. Add the tomato paste, plus an equal amount of water, and bring to a boil. Simmer for about 10 minutes, then add the tomatoes. Return it to a boil, then simmer for at least 30 minutes. Add the Italian seasoning, sugar, pepper, and brandy. Cook for about 10 minutes. Check for seasoning. Serve with spaghetti.

Serves 5 or 6

Most people have learned to make spaghetti sauce, but many have difficulty getting the acidity out of it. Some use baking soda, others an overabundance of sugar, still others wine by the cupful. My way, I guarantee no acid!

SPAGHETTI WITH WHITE CLAM SAUCE

6	tablespoons olive oil	2	large pinches of basil
6	garlic cloves, chopped	2	large pinches of oregano
24 to 32	shucked clams, liquor reserved, or 1 medium can		Pepper
			Chopped fresh parsley

*H*eat a large skillet, add the oil, and heat it. Add the garlic and sauté very lightly, not permitting it to turn brown. Add the shucked clams and sauté them for just a few minutes, then add the seasonings, cook a bit, and add the reserved clam liquor. (If the clams are canned, add them and their liquor along with the basil, then the oregano, and finally the pepper.) Serve with a thin-style spaghetti. Top with parsley.
Serves 4

Variation: Spaghetti with Red Clam Sauce. Add a cup of spaghetti sauce.

SPAGHETTI WITH GARLIC AND OIL

1¹/₂	pounds spaghetti	8	plus garlic cloves
¹/₂	cup olive oil		Pepper
1	small onion, finely minced	¹/₂	cup finely chopped fresh parsley

*C*ook the spaghetti and set aside. Keep warm. Heat a skillet, add the oil, and heat it. Add the onion and sauté until clarified. Add the garlic and sauté it to a very light golden color. Add the pepper and parsley, heat through, and serve immediately over the spaghetti.
Serves 6

THE CLASSIC FETTUCCINE ALFREDO

1	pound wide fettuccine noodles	4	sticks (2 cups) butter, cut into small pieces
1	pound Parmesan cheese		

*C*ook the noodles until just done; drain. Add half of the butter and toss to melt it. Grate in half of the cheese and toss all together in a large heatproof bowl. Bake in a preheated 400° oven for 5 minutes. Remove, add the remaining butter, grate in the remaining cheese, and serve, as is. This is the only true fettuccine Alfredo, although today it is often made with cream added.

Serves 4

STUFFED SHELLS THE EASY WAY

1	garlic clove, crushed	3	eggs, well beaten
	Large pasta shells (4 per person)	6	tablespoons chopped fresh parsley
1½	pounds ricotta cheese	6	tablespoons grated Romano cheese
¼	cup heavy cream		White pepper
2	tablespoons Italian dry white wine		

*H*eat a large pot of water with the garlic in it. Cook the shells only until they become somewhat rubbery, *not al dente,* for they will be cooked further in the oven. Mix all of the other ingredients together and use to stuff the shells. Place them in a large oven pan, pour in a little water (or some of the sauce you will be serving), cover the pan, and bake in a preheated 325° oven for 15 minutes. Uncover the pan and give it but 5 minutes more. Serve with sauce—white, cheese, or tomato.

Serves 6 to 8

Variation: Shells with Meat Stuffing.

1	cup ground Italian ham
¼	cup ground chicken or veal
½	teaspoon grated lemon zest
½	pound ricotta cheese
2	eggs, well beaten
⅛	teaspoon grated nutmeg
1	cup soft bread crumbs
2	tablespoons finely chopped fresh parsley

*M*ix together and use to stuff the shells.

MONTERREY PLAZA'S SAFFRON TAGLIATELLE WITH SHRIMP

2	tablespoons shallots	1	pound saffron-flavored tagliatelle, cooked
1	tablespoon olive oil		
1	very large tomato, peeled and seeded	4	tablespoons butter
		2	tablespoons chopped fresh parsley
6	ounces dry white wine		Salt
4	ounces fish stock		Pepper
12	ounces bay shrimp		

*S*auté the shallots in oil; add the tomato, wine, and fish stock. Reduce by one half. Add the shrimp and cook until done. Add the tagliatelle and bring to a boil. Remove from the heat and stir in the butter, parsley, and salt and pepper to taste.
Serves 4

I was given this recipe by chef Steve Pagano at the Monterrey Plaza when I was a guest there in 1986. To me, it's one of the classiest luncheon dishes of all time.

VERMICELLI WITH RICOTTA CHEESE

1	cup milk		Salt
1	pound ricotta cheese		Pepper
2	tablespoons butter	1	pound vermicelli
4	tablespoons grated Parmesan cheese		

*W*arm the milk, add the ricotta, and cream them together. Add the butter, half of the Parmesan cheese, and salt and pepper. Cook the vermicelli, then mix with the cheese sauce. Serve with a light sprinkling of the remaining Parmesan cheese.
Serves 4

THREE-CHEESE PASTA

	Italian seasoned bread crumbs	4	ounces Swiss cheese, chopped
1	pound egg noodle bows	4	ounces mozzarella cheese, chopped
2	tablespoons butter		
4	ounces freshly grated Parmesan cheese	4	cups béchamel sauce (page 242)

*B*utter a large casserole dish and sprinkle with bread crumbs. Cook the noodles and toss with the butter and cheeses. Place half of the mixture in the casserole dish and top with half of the béchamel sauce. Put the rest of the mixture in the casserole dish and pour the remaining sauce over it. Top with a light coating of bread crumbs and bake in a preheated 350° oven for 15 to 20 minutes, being careful not to burn the top.

Serves 4

PASTA AND PEAS

1	pound curly pasta		Salt
4	tablespoons olive oil		Pepper
4	garlic cloves, crushed	1¹/₂	cups frozen peas
1	1-pound 12-ounce can plum tomatoes, crushed		

*C*ook the pasta *al dente*. Heat the oil in a skillet and sauté the garlic. Add the tomatoes, salt, and pepper. Bring to a boil, turn the heat down to a simmer, add the peas, and heat through. Serve over the pasta. You can serve grated cheese with it, if you like.

Serves 4

Variation: Omit the tomatoes and add 6 mushrooms, chopped, and 6 ounces grated mozzarella cheese.

PASTA WITH MUSHROOMS AND PEAS

1	pound thin spaghetti	1	10-ounce package frozen peas, thawed
2 to 3	tablespoons olive oil	8	slices bacon, cooked and crumbled
2 to 3	tablespoons bacon fat		Pepper
12	mushrooms, thinly sliced	1/2	cup grated Parmesan cheese

*B*reak the spaghetti into 1- to 2-inch pieces. Cook and set aside. Add olive oil to the bacon fat in a skillet, heat, and sauté the mushrooms until cooked. Add the peas and just heat through. Mix in the spaghetti, bacon, and pepper. Serve with a sprinkling of Parmesan cheese.

Serves 4

PASTA PRIMAREDA

Dressing

1/2	cup red wine vinegar	3	tablespoons olive oil
1	teaspoon minced garlic	1	each green and red pepper, seeded and finely minced
1	large onion, grated		
3	tablespoons each chopped fresh sweet basil and dill, or 1 tablespoon each dried	1	tablespoon Italian seasoning
		1	tablespoon ground caraway seeds
1	teaspoon pepper		

1 package rotini noodles (three colors—made with egg, spinach, and carrots)

24 to 36	thumb-size florets mixed broccoli and cauliflower	1	pound very small shrimp, peeled and deveined
1	pound chicken meat, cut into bite-size pieces	8	ounces mozzarella cheese, sliced or grated

*P*ut all of the dressing ingredients in a pot, bring to a boil, turn the heat down to a simmer, and cook for just a few minutes. Set aside and keep warm.

Cook the noodles *al dente.* Steam the florets. Sauté the chicken. Cook the shrimp. Mix together with the dressing, add the cheese, and serve.

Serves 4

PASTA PRIMAVEGA

1	package curly pasta	6	large mushrooms, sliced
6	scallions, chopped	2	celery stalks, chopped
1	large cucumber, peeled, seeded, and diced	1	red onion, chopped
		1	yellow onion, chopped
1	each green and red pepper, seeded and chopped	2	large carrots, chopped
		4	radishes, sliced
		1	large zucchini, diced

Seasoning Mixture

4	tablespoons olive oil	4	garlic cloves
1	large onion	1	tablespoon pepper
10	tablespoons chopped fresh sweet basil or 4 tablespoons dried	2	tablespoons rosemary
		1/2	cup white wine vinegar
1	tablespoon ground coriander	2	tomatoes, chopped
1	tablespoon dark soy sauce		

Cook the pasta and keep warm. Steam the vegetables, starting with the one that takes longest to cook. Cook the seasonings together; add the tomatoes last and just let them warm through. Combine everything in a large mixing bowl and serve.

Serves 4

Note: Instead of the seasoning mixture you can use a packaged seasoning mix. Also, the dish can be served cold, too.

CHICKEN AND PEANUTS WITH LONG-LIFE NOODLES

1/4	cup peanut oil	6	scallions, chopped
1	cup raw peanuts	1	can sliced water chestnuts
1	pound sliced cooked chicken meat	2	tablespoons sherry
1	can bamboo shoots		Pepper
2	tablespoons dark soy sauce	1	pound egg noodles

Heat the oil in a preheated wok or skillet and cook the peanuts until just slightly browned. Remove and chop. Return them to the pan and add all of the remaining ingredients, except the noodles. Sauté lightly to heat through. Cook the noodles and place on a large serving platter. Cover with the chicken mixture.

Serves 6

There are several types of Chinese noodles, such as cellophane noodles, sometimes called Chinese vermicelli or bean thread; fresh noodles, called lo mein, made with eggs; yee fu noodles, a fried dried egg noodle. At feasts, most dishes are usually served with noodles, often of great length, for the Chinese have always regarded the noodle as a symbol of longevity.

This recipe shows how you can make a large number of dishes from one basic method of preparation. A wok is the ideal utensil, but you can use a large skillet and accomplish the same result.

JAPANESE NOODLES AND PORK IN BROWN SAUCE

4	dried mushrooms	1/2	tablespoon hoisin sauce
1 1/2	tablespoons brown bean sauce	2	tablespoons sake
1/2	garlic clove, finely minced	1/2	tablespoon dark soy sauce
1/2	teaspoon sugar	1/2	pound fresh noodles
1	slice ginger root, finely minced	1 1/2	tablespoons peanut oil
8	ounces ground pork		

Soak the mushrooms in water for at least 1 hour, then slice them thin. Mix the bean sauce, garlic, sugar, and ginger, and in another bowl mix the pork, hoisin sauce, sake, and soy sauce. Set aside. Cook the noodles and set aside to keep warm. Heat the oil in a large skillet, add the bean sauce mixture and mushrooms, and stir-fry very quickly. Add the pork mixture and stir-fry until the pork is well cooked. If it seems somewhat dry, add about 1/4 cup water, cover the skillet, and cook for another 5 to 6 minutes. Place the noodles on a very large platter and serve the sauced pork over it.

Serves 4

RICE

*R*ice is one of the most diversified of foods. Although the Far East is supposedly where rice is king, more varieties are grown in this country. The usual basic division is into long-grain and short-grain. Long-grain rice is long and narrow. Short-grain rice is most commonly used by those for whom rice is a mainstay.

BOILED RICE

1 cup raw long-grain rice   2 cups water

*W*ash the rice under running water until the water runs clear. Put it in a saucepan with the 2 cups water. Cover lightly and bring to a boil over high heat. Reduce the heat to its lowest point and cook for 20 minutes.
Serves 6

GRAHAM KERR'S STEAMED RICE

5/8 cup long-grain rice   1 tablespoon salt
3 pints water

*W*ash the rice under cold water until no color shows in the runoff. Put the 3 pints water in a pot, add the salt, and bring to a boil. Let the rice fall in a bit at a time; let it boil for 10 minutes. Drain the rice in a metal colander, and set the colander on top of a saucepan with a small amount of water in it. Place a lid over the rice and steam it for 8 minutes. Fluff it up with a fork.
Serves 6 to 8

This is the very best steamed rice I have ever tried, thanks to my good friend Graham Kerr, the former Galloping Gourmet.

INDIAN YELLOW RICE

1 cup raw long-grain   2 1/2 cups chicken stock
    rice   1/8 teaspoon powdered
3 tablespoons butter   saffron

*I*n a 4-quart pot, sauté the rice in butter until it turns a light golden brown. Heat the chicken stock, add the saffron, and add this to the rice. Bring it to a boil again, set on simmer, and cook for about 30 minutes, being certain not to disturb it during that time.

Serves 6

YELLOW RICE PILAF

2½	cups chicken stock	1	red and 1 green pepper, seeded and coarsely chopped
	Several drops yellow food coloring		
1	cup raw rice	1	large onion, coarsely chopped
8	tablespoons (1 stick) butter	8	mushrooms, thinly sliced

*H*eat the chicken stock and add food coloring to make it a very rich yellow. Put in the rice and bring to a boil. Let it boil for 1 minute, then let it simmer, covered, for about 20 minutes. Check for doneness—stir it with a fork, and cook a bit longer if it is not done. When it is, set it aside. Heat a large skillet, melt the butter in it, and sauté the peppers and onion until almost finished. Add the mushrooms, cook them slightly, then add the rice and stir well.

Serves 6 to 8

Variation: Ann's Orzo Pilaf. Use orzo instead of rice, and do not cook it as long.

ORIENTAL HAWAIIAN FRUIT PILAF

3	ounces each dried figs, prunes, apricots, peaches, and dates	1	cup raw brown rice
1/4	cup fresh dates	1/2	teaspoon ground cinnamon
1/4	cup seedless raisins	1/4	cup pine nuts
1/4	cup each Madeira and plum wine		Butter
		1/4	cup chopped almonds

Soak the dried fruit in hot water for 1 hour. Drain, reserving the water. Marinate them, along with the fresh dates and raisins, in the wines for 30 minutes to 4 hours. Drain; measure the reserved soaking water and wine and add enough water to make 4 cups. Cook the rice in it. Keep in mind that it does take longer (up to 45 minutes) to cook brown rice than white rice. When the rice is done, stir in the cinammon and pine nuts. Put the rice in a buttered casserole, dot with butter, and bake in a preheated 350° oven for 10 minutes. Mix in the marinated fruit and garnish with the almonds.

Serves 6

Note: When you open a jar of pine nuts, refrigerate the unused part, as they quickly turn rancid.

POLYNESIAN GREEN RICE

3	tablespoons chopped scallions, green part only	1/4	cup chopped fresh parsley
2 1/2	tablespoons butter	6	ounces chopped almonds
1 1/2	tablespoons curry powder	1	large pimiento, finely chopped
	Salt	12	large spinach leaves
1 1/2	cups cooked rice	1/4	cup water
		2	tablespoons rice wine

Sauté the scallions in the butter with the curry powder and just a dash of salt. Add to the rice, along with the parsley, almonds, and pimiento. Mix well. Put a large spoonful of this

on each spinach leaf and roll up. Place the leaves in a large baking pan, add the water and wine, cover the pan, and bake in a preheated 400° oven for 30 minutes.
Serves 4

SPANISH RICE

1/2	pound bacon	1	1-pound 4-ounce can
1	cup raw rice		tomatoes
1/2	cup chopped onion	1/4	cup chili sauce
1/2	cup chopped green	1	teaspoon salt
	pepper	1/2	teaspoon pepper

*C*hop the bacon into small pieces and cook in a large skillet. Remove the bacon, crumble it, and reserve. Leave the drippings in the skillet and sauté the rice, onion, and green pepper. Add the bacon and remaining ingredients, along with a tomato-can-ful of water, cover, and simmer for at least 45 minutes, until the rice is tender. Make sure everything is well mixed.
Serves 6

RICE STUFFING FOR TOMATOES, ZUCCHINI, OR EGGPLANT

1	cup raw rice	1/2	tablespoon sugar
1/2	cup olive oil		Salt
1	medium onion, thinly sliced		Pepper
1	large tomato, peeled and chopped	2	tablespoons chopped fresh parsley
2	tablespoons pine nuts	2	tablespoons chopped fresh dill
2	tablespoons dried currants, soaked in water for at least 30 minutes and drained	1/2	tablespoon thyme
		6	tomatoes, zucchini, or eggplants, hollowed out

*W*ash the rice well and let it drain. In a very deep pan, heat the olive oil and fry the onion until soft. Add the chopped tomato, nuts, currants, sugar, salt, pepper, parsley, dill, and thyme. Stir in the rice and fry for 2 to 3 minutes. Add water to cover by 1/2 inch. Cover the pan and boil for 20 minutes, then only until the water is absorbed. Remove from the heat and let set for a few minutes. Uncover and let cool. Use the mixture to stuff the vegetables. Put them in a pan with a bit of water in the bottom. Bake, uncovered, at 350° for about 45 minutes, until they feel tender and done to your satisfaction.

Serves 6

RICE CROQUETTES

61/2 tablespoons butter	Wash: milk, cream, or
1/4 cup flour	beaten egg
21/4 cups milk, heated	Cracker crumbs
almost to a simmer	mixed with finely
11/2 teaspoons salt	crushed nuts or
1/2 teaspoon nutmeg	very finely chopped
1/8 teaspoon white	dried raisins or
pepper	prunes or fresh
3 cups cooked rice	dates
5 egg yolks, beaten	

*M*elt the butter in a saucepan, stir in the flour, and cook carefully, stirring, for a few minutes; do not let it brown. Add the milk gradually, stirring until it thickens and is smooth. Add the salt, nutmeg, pepper, and rice. Cook, stirring, until the mixture boils at the sides of the pan and leaves the bottom of the pan easily. A spoonful at a time, add 4 to 5 tablespoons of the hot rice mixture to the egg yolks, stirring constantly, then incorporate the egg yolks into the rice. Turn the mixture out onto a well-buttered flat pan, and cover with wax paper or greased paper to keep it from crusting. Let cool and refrigerate, to make it easier to handle. When it is cold, use an ice cream scoop for portions the size of an egg. Roll them into the desired shape, bread them, and fry in deep fat at 350° until golden brown.

Serves 6

VEGETABLE-RICE MEDLEY

3	cups chicken stock	8	florets each broccoli and cauliflower, each cut into 4 pieces
1	large green pepper, seeded and dried		
1	large red pepper, seeded and diced	6	scallions, green part only, finely chopped
1	large yellow onion, chopped	2	carrots, cut into small dice
8	mushrooms, thinly sliced	2	cups cooked rice Pepper

*H*eat the chicken stock in a large pot and cook all of the vegetables. Drain, reserving the stock. Mix the rice with the cooked vegetables and season to taste. If the dish appears too dry, add just enough of the stock to make it slightly moist but not wet.
Serves 6

BAKED RICE AND CARROTS

6	slices bacon, diced	1½	cups finely diced carrots
4	scallions, white part only, finely chopped	3	cups cooked rice Salt Pepper
6	mushrooms, thinly sliced	1	cup heavy cream
		2	eggs, beaten

*C*ook the bacon, set aside, and sauté the scallions and then the mushrooms in the bacon drippings. Blanch the carrots in hot water for only a few minutes. Drain. Mix together all of the ingredients, except the cream and eggs. Put in a buttered large casserole. Whip the cream until fluffy and add the eggs. Fold into the rice mixture. Bake, covered, at 325° for at least 45 minutes. Remove the cover and, if need be, bake until the top is a light golden brown.
Serves 6

PORK FRIED RICE

8 ounces pork, finely
  chopped
1 onion, finely chopped
1/2 each green and red
  pepper, seeded and
  finely chopped
3 scallions, finely
  chopped
1 tablespoon light soy
  sauce

1 tablespoon dark soy
  sauce
1 tablespoon hoisin
  sauce
Pepper
3 cups cooked rice
1/4 cup pork stock
  (optional)

*I*n a heated skillet, cook the pork, then add the onion, green and red peppers, and scallions. Sauté for a few minutes; add the light and dark soy sauce and hoisin sauce. Season with pepper, add the rice, and heat through. If the mixture is too dry, add some pork stock. Toss all of this together and serve.

Serves 4

FRIED RICE, JAPANESE STYLE

2 tablespoons oil
6 small mushrooms
6 scallions, chopped
1 tablespoon dark soy
  sauce

2 tablespoons sake
1 1/2 cups cooked rice
2 eggs, beaten

*H*eat the skillet, heat the oil in it, add the mushrooms, scallions, soy sauce, and sake, and cook for a few minutes. Do not overcook it. Add the rice, stir well, and cook for 5 minutes or so. Add the eggs and cook, stirring, for a few minutes longer.

Serves 4

HOPPIN' JOHN

2 cups black-eyed peas	2 large pimientos, cut
4 ounces somewhat lean	into medium dice
bacon or salt pork,	Salt
cut into small pieces	Pepper
3 cups cooked rice	

*S*oak the peas overnight. Rinse them and put in a pot with about 1 quart water, along with the bacon or salt pork. Cook very slowly for at least 1 hour. Check for doneness. Add the rice and pimientos and season to taste.

Serves 6

Strictly southern style.

WILD RICE STUFFING

Fat from a wild goose,	8 ounces pork sausage
duck, or other wild	meat
bird, even turkey	1/2 Granny Smith apple,
1/2 large onion, finely	cored and chopped
chopped	1/2 cup cooked wild rice
1 celery stalk, finely	1 cup cooked brown rice
chopped	About 2 pinches of
	poultry seasoning

*R*ender the fat from the bird and sauté the onion and celery in it. Drain off the fat. Break up the sausage and cook it in the pan with the onion and celery. When it is done, add the apple and cook until it is soft. Add the wild rice and brown rice, mix well, and season to taste.

Serves 4

Variation: Use bacon instead of sausage and add sautéed sliced mushrooms.

Wild rice (actually, not rice but a perennial grass native to North America) is harvested by hand by the Indians of Minnesota.

SALADS

*T*here are as many variations as there are types of ingredients. You can add almost anything to a salad, or change it by varying the dressing (see pages 261–64.

It is true that romaine lettuce should be used for Caesar salad, but it is not gospel. If it is not available, use another. So what? There is Boston lettuce, iceberg, bibb, leaf, or even escarole. How about endive? Who says you can't use it? It's more expensive than the others, but you can still use it. A great many people like a more bitter type of green—kale, dandelion greens, spinach, or any other of the many mustard or sour grass types.

Learning to mix all sorts of vegetables with greens and dressings is the only thing you have to do. Use peppers—hot, mild, sweet, or even sour—tomatoes, eggs, radishes, celery, cabbages, and so on.

CHEF'S SALAD

1 head lettuce	1 dill pickle, cut
8 ounces ham	lengthwise into 4
2 green peppers, seeded	slices
and sliced into strips	4 slices American cheese
4 mushrooms, thinly	4 slices Swiss cheese
sliced	1 pound turkey meat
8 black olives	4 hard-boiled eggs

*U*sing lettuce as a base, mound the salad by arranging all of the ingredients decoratively. Top with a dressing of your choice.

Serves 4

CAESAR SALAD

1/2 cup salad oil	1 large head romaine
1 tablespoon	lettuce
Worcestershire sauce	1/2 cup crumbled blue
3/4 teaspoon salt	cheese
1/2 teaspoon pepper	1/4 cup freshly grated
2 lemons	Parmesan cheese
2 garlic cloves, cut in	1 egg
half	2 cups croutons
4 anchovies	

*C*ombine the oil with the Worcestershire sauce, salt, pepper, and juice of 1/2 lemon. Set aside. Completely crush the garlic in the bottom of a large wooden bowl, rubbing it into the bowl with as much force as possible. Likewise, crush and rub in the anchovies. Break the romaine into nice bite-size pieces (do not cut it). Toss with the garlic and anchovies, sprinkle in the cheeses, pour in the dressing, and toss again. Break the egg over this. Drip on the juice of the remaining 11/2 lemons and then toss to mix well. Top with the croutons, toss once again, and serve.

Serves 4

SPINACH SALAD

1/4 cup Italian dressing
(page 262, or use
bottled dressing)
1/4 cup French dressing
(page 262)
1/2 cup mayonnaise
1/2 tablespoon lemon juice
1 garlic clove, crushed
Salt

Pepper
2 bunches or 1 package
spinach, washed and
torn into pieces
2 eggs, hard-boiled, and
chopped
4 slices bacon, cooked
and crumbled
4 mushrooms, sliced

Combine the dressings, mayonnaise, lemon juice, garlic, salt, and pepper and mix well. Pour over the spinach and toss. Sprinkle the eggs, bacon, and mushrooms over each portion.
Serves 4

HOT SPINACH-FETA-RICOTTA CHEESE

1 1/2 pounds fresh spinach
or 1 pound frozen
spinach, thawed
and well drained
4 tablespoons olive oil
2 garlic cloves, minced
1 large onion, chopped
2 jiggers dry vermouth

Salt
Pepper
10 ounces ricotta cheese
10 ounces feta cheese,
crumbled
4 tablespoons chopped
fresh parsley

If the spinach is fresh, wash it, break it up into small pieces, and sauté in oil with garlic and onion. When done, season with the vermouth, salt, and pepper. If the spinach is frozen, add the seasonings to it *before* sautéing.
Put the spinach in a large casserole dish. Mix the two cheeses with the parsley and place on top of the spinach. Bake in a preheated 360° oven until the cheese becomes golden brown.
Serves 4

CREOLE RICE SALAD

4 tablespoons olive oil
2 garlic cloves, minced
2 large pinches of Paul
   Prudhomme's
   Seafood Magic
   Seasoning
1/4 teaspoon Tabasco
   sauce
6 scallions, chopped
8 ounces chopped ham

12 ounces cooked
   shrimp, peeled,
   deveined, and cut
   into pieces
1 green pepper, seeded
   and chopped
3 cups cooked rice
3 tomatoes, chopped
   Leaf lettuce

*I*n a blender, mix the oil, garlic, seafood seasoning, and Tabasco sauce. Place in a bowl and add the scallions, ham, shrimp, and green pepper. Mix well. Add the rice, mix, and chill until quite cool. Mix in the tomatoes and serve on a bed of lettuce.
   Serves 4

Aspic and Gelatin Salads

A gelatin salad takes its flavor from the ingredients, rather than from the gelatin. Thus, you can make a gelatin salad by cutting up, say, fruit, cooking it in fruit juice and gelatin (softened in cold water), and pouring the mixture into a mold and chilling it. Roll the outside of the mold in hot water to loosen the salad, then turn it out onto a serving dish. Top it with a brandied cream sauce: whipped cream, sour cream, a bit of yogurt, and brandy (or bourbon), mixed to the desired consistency.

Aspic is made from a concentrated stock, which gels from the proteins extracted during cooking. If it is not firm enough —aspic from fish stock, for example—softened powdered gelatin can be added. Aspics can also be made from flavorful liquids such as tomato juice, as in the following recipe.

SHRIMP ASPIC SALAD

1	package unflavored gelatin	2	celery stalks, cut into 1-inch dice
12	shrimp, peeled and deveined	1	pint tomato juice
1/2	large onion, cut into 1-inch dice	4	tablespoons Chablis
		1	teaspoon tarragon
		1	tablespoon lemon juice

*P*repare the gelatin according to the directions on the envelope. Heat all of the remaining ingredients together until the shrimp are cooked. Combine with the gelatin, pour into a mold, and refrigerate until firm. Dip the outside of the mold in hot water and invert onto a serving dish.
Serves 4

WILLIAM'S CHEESE SALAD

6	ounces cream cheese	2	tablespoons unflavored gelatin, softened in cold water
1	cup light cream		
1/4	cup ground almonds	1	tablespoon tarragon vinegar
1/4	cup chopped cashews		
1/4	cup cold milk	3/4	cup heavy cream
		1	bunch watercress

*P*ut the cream cheese and light cream in a double boiler and cook until completely blended, stirring often. Add the almonds and cashews. Combine the milk and gelatin. Add it to the cheese mixture and stir until completely incorporated. Let cool. Stir in the vinegar. Beat the heavy cream and fold it into the cheese mixture. Place in a mold, such as a ring mold, and chill. Unmold and serve on a bed of watercress, or with the watercress around the edges of the salad.
Serves 6

Eggs and Egg Dishes

*W*ith all the cooking that is done with eggs, the general public knows so little about them that it is almost sinful. I will try to give you some of the pertinent facts concerning eggs.

Eggs are graded by weight, but the important thing is their freshness. They are further graded by flavor and appearance: grades AA to C—the best to the worst.

AA is an egg that is less than 24 hours old when it reaches the store, and and it is heavy; a dozen of these eggs weigh about 2 pounds. It is said that all grade AA and A eggs are okay for eating as is; grades B and C should be used only for baking. What is the distinction between B and C? I don't know—but I can tell you how to ascertain whether an egg is fresh or old.

Obviously, you cannot candle an egg at the store. Instead, hold it by your ear and shake it. A fresh egg just about fills the shell; as it grows older, the amount of albumen (white) shrinks. So if you hear very little sloshing, you know it is fairly fresh. If you hear a great deal of sloshing, put it back—it is too old.

Color does not have any bearing on the egg's nutritional value or its freshness. You may have heard that white eggs usually are stored for shipment and brown eggs are from local farmers only. Not true.

Eggshells are very porous, so odors can permeate the inside under poor storage conditions. Therefore, they should always be kept covered in your refrigerator.

Now that you have that down pat, let us get to cooking techniques. There are so many ways to cook eggs that people are often confused, but it's a simple thing to learn (as are most things in cooking).

Never cook eggs directly from the refrigerator. Allow them to reach room temperature, especially if you are going to cook them in the shell. Have you ever had them crack after you put them in the water? The cause is the shock of going from ice cold to boiling hot. At room temperature they will react well to any cooking technique.

Never boil eggs. To cook "hard-boiled" eggs, bring the water to a boil and then turn the heat down to a simmer.

Poaching eggs is not difficult, but you may have had trouble with the albumen spreading over the pan. Add a bit of vinegar to the water before putting in the egg. It will not affect the taste, but will keep the white from spreading.

Coddling eggs is done in special dishes, and the egg is cooked at just below the boiling point—nothing more, nothing less.

Shirred eggs are done in two ways. First, place an egg in a buttered shirred egg dish and cook it slowly on top of the stove until the white just begins to set, then transfer to a preheated 360° oven and finish cooking. Never overcook, for the purpose of shirring eggs is to serve them soft, not hard. The second way of preparing them is to butter the shirred dish, place the egg in it, and bake at 360° from start to finish.

There is no trick to making good scrambled eggs. Just follow this simple rule: not too hot, not too fast.

OMELETTE

3   eggs
1   ounce water

Butter

Sample Fillings

Jelly
Lox, cream cheese, and dill
Crab meat
Sautéed shrimp and garlic

Sautéed mushrooms and
    onions
Grated cheese
Assorted blanched
    vegetables

*B*eat the eggs and water thoroughly. Heat an omelette pan
with a light coating of butter to high heat. Add the eggs and
allow them to start to set. Stir slightly, pulling up the edges so
liquid egg can run underneath. Add the filling. Place the pan
under a broiler until the omelette fluffs. Fold the omelette and
remove it to a plate.
    Serves 1

*Use room-temperature eggs to make the omelette fluffy. Make sure the
omelette pan has a heatproof handle that can go under the broiler or in
the oven.*

FRENCH-STYLE OMELETTE

6   eggs
    Salt
    Pepper
1/2   cup milk

2   tablespoons butter
    Filling (type and
        amount to taste)

*B*eat the eggs just enough to blend the whites and yolks. Stir in the salt, pepper, and milk. Melt the butter in a large skillet over low heat. When it just begins to bubble, pour in the egg mixture. Cook for a minute or so, until the edges start to firm up. Keep lifting the edges and letting the liquid pour under to continue cooking. When it is evenly cooked, add your filling— diced ham, pieces of cooked chicken, slices of cheese, or any type of jam or jelly. Fold it over, heat through, and serve.
Serves 2

CAVIAR OMELETTE

4	eggs, separated	1	tablespoon chopped chives
3	tablespoons hot water		
1/2	teaspoon salt	2	tablespoons caviar
	Butter	2	tablespoons sour cream

*B*eat the egg yolks until light in color, then add the hot water and salt. Beat the egg whites until very stiff and fold them in. Butter an omelette pan well and heat it slightly. Pour in the omelette mixture and cook over a low flame until it sets (firms up). Put it under the broiler until golden but not too brown. Mix the chives, caviar, and sour cream into a loose but spreadable paste. Spread over the top of the omelette, fold it in half, and broil to a light golden color. Serve immediately. I like it with hollandaise sauce on top and potato pancakes.
Serves 2

A SPANISH OMELETTE OF CLASS

1	cup coarsely chopped onions	1	tablespoon minced fresh parsley
6	tablespoons butter	1/2	teaspoon salt (optional)
1/2	cup chopped cooked ham	1/2	cup white wine
1	cup canned tomatoes	1	cup cooked small shrimp
		6	eggs, beaten

*S*auté the onions in 4 tablespoons butter. Add the ham and tomatoes, parsley, salt, and wine. Set aside. Just before you are ready to add the mixture to the omelette, add the shrimp and heat through. Melt the remaining butter in a large skillet with a tight-fitting lid. Add the eggs, cover, and cook to let the bottom brown slightly. Turn and do the other side. Serve with the filling on top.

Serves 2

A GOURMET'S OMELETTE

1/3	cup plus 4 tablespoons butter		Meat from 1 1-pound lobster
1/3	cup flour	6	eggs, separated
1 1/2	cups milk	2	tablespoons parsley sprigs
1/2	teaspoon salt		

*M*elt the 1/3 cup butter in top of a double boiler; stir in the flour until it is smoothly blended. Add the milk and salt and place over boiling water. Cook, stirring constantly, until the mixture has thickened. Remove two thirds of the sauce and set aside to cool to room temperature. Add the lobster meat to the sauce in the double boiler and keep warm.

Beat the egg yolks until lightly colored and slightly thickened; add the cooled white sauce and heat to mix thoroughly. Beat the egg whites until stiff. Fold them into the egg yolk–cream mixture. Butter the inside of the lid of a 10-inch skillet and melt the remaining butter in the skillet. Pour in the egg mixture, smooth the top with a rubber spatula or a spoon, and cover the skillet. Cook over low heat for 15 minutes, or until the sides and the bottom of the omelette have turned a light golden brown and it has puffed up and cooked through.

Cut through the center with a sharp knife to within 1/2 inch of the bottom, loosen the omelette, and transfer it to a heated platter. Pour the lobster sauce over half the omelette and fold over the other half. Garnish with parsley.
Serves 2

APRICOT SOUFFLÉ OMELETTE

2	eggs, separated	1	tablespoon butter
1	tablespoon superfine sugar, plus extra for garnish	6	ounces hot cooked or canned apricot halves (3 to 4 whole apricots)

*I*n a mixing bowl, with a wooden spoon beat the egg yolks, sugar, and 2 teaspoons water until creamy. Whisk the egg whites to the stiff-peaks stage. Gently fold them into the yolks.

Heat the butter in a 6- to 7-inch omelette pan until very hot. Add the eggs and cook until golden brown underneath. Put the pan under a hot grill and lightly brown the top of the omelette. Slide the omelette onto a heated serving plate and place the hot apricots on half of it. Fold over the other half and dust the top with the extra sugar.
Serves 1

SCRAMBLED EGGS, FRENCH STYLE

8	tablespoons (1 stick) butter	Pepper
12	eggs, slightly beaten Salt	About 1/2 cup heavy cream

*M*elt half of the butter in a very large skillet. Slowly add the eggs to the pan and, stirring with a wooden fork or spoon, cook over low heat until the eggs are firm but not hard. Remove the pan from the heat. Put the remaining butter and the salt and pepper in the pan, and stir in just enough cream to make the dish rich. (If the eggs are very fresh, they will absorb most, if not all, of the suggested amounts of butter and cream.)

Serves 4

EGGS BENEDICT

8	slices (about 1 pound) Canadian bacon, sliced 1/8 inch thick	8	poached eggs
		1/2	pint hollandaise sauce (page 245)
4	English muffins, split and toasted	8	black olives
			Parsley

*B*roil the bacon slightly, but do not dry it out with too much heat. Place a slice of bacon on each English muffin half. Top with a poached egg. Ladle 1 ounce of hollandaise sauce over each egg. Decorate the egg with a slice of black olive and garnish the plate with parsley.

Serves 4

BASIC SOUFFLÉ

3	eggs, separated, plus 3 egg whites	1/3	cup milk
			Salt
4	tablespoons melted butter		Pepper
1	teaspoon plus sherry	1	cup grated cheddar or other cheese
1/4	cup sifted flour		

*I*n a mixing bowl large enough to hold all of the ingredients, whip the egg yolks with the melted butter, sherry, flour, milk, salt, and pepper. If it seems too thick, add a bit more milk.

In another bowl, whip the egg whites until they reach the soft-peaks stage; don't make them too stiff. Add the cheese and mix again, then fold into the egg yolk mixture. Pour into a 1 1/2- to 2-quart soufflé dish and set it in a pan of hot water. Bake on the middle shelf of a preheated 400° oven for at least 1 hour, until it has risen 1 1/2 to 2 inches over the top. Serve it as soon as possible, for it will fall; they always do.

Serves 4

Note: Caution! Never open the oven door during the cooking process. If you do, it will fall before you can serve it.

Variation: Chocolate and Brandy Soufflé. Substitute sweet chocolate for the cheese and use a good coffee brandy with it.

Soufflés are very easy to make. The basic ingredients are always egg whites, a liquid mixture of egg yolks and flavorings, butter, and flour. The liquid ingredients should always be about one third of the amount of the whites. You can add almost anything to the liquid mixture to make the soufflé of your choice, such as brandy or cognac, chocolate, cheese, or strawberries. Follow these simple rules and impress your friends.

BROCCOLI SOUFFLÉ

1/2 cup mayonnaise
1/4 cup sifted flour
1 1/2 cups milk
1 teaspoon salt
Small amount of white pepper

6 tablespoons grated cheese
4 eggs, separated
1 10-ounce package frozen broccoli, thawed and drained

Combine the mayonnaise and flour and mix well. Heat it slowly, and slowly add the milk; stir constantly until thick. Add the salt, pepper, and cheese. Cook again for a short time. Let cool. Beat the egg yolks and stir them in, along with the broccoli. Beat the egg whites until stiff and fold them in. Pour into a buttered 1 1/2- to 2-quart soufflé dish and set it in a pan of hot water. Bake in a preheated 300° oven for 1 hour and 15 minutes.

Serves 4

Variations: Omit the salt and add 4 to 6 ounces chopped cooked ham. Replace the broccoli with any other vegetable you like.

SPINACH SOUFFLÉ

1	tablespoon grated Parmesan cheese	2	tablespoons lemon juice
7 to 8	tablespoons butter	5	tablespoons flour
2 or 3	shallots, minced	1 1/2	cups milk
1	10-ounce package frozen chopped spinach, thawed and drained	1	teaspoon salt
			White pepper
		6	eggs, separated, plus 1 egg white

*P*reheat the oven to 400°. Ordinarily you don't butter a soufflé dish, because it prevents the soufflé from rising up the sides of the dish, but for this soufflé butter a 2-quart soufflé dish and sprinkle the bottom and sides with the Parmesan cheese.

Melt 1 tablespoon butter in a heavy saucepan and sauté the shallots for 2 to 3 minutes. Add the spinach and lemon juice and cook over very low heat, stirring frequently, until all of the liquid has evaporated. This should take about 10 minutes. Set aside.

Melt the remaining butter in a heavy saucepan and, over low heat, stir in the flour with a wire whisk; remove from the heat. Bring the milk to a boil and add it to the butter-flour mixture. Whisk until very smooth. Add the salt and pepper and continue whisking until well blended. Let this white sauce cool a little. Beat the egg yolks into the sauce, one at a time. Stir in the spinach and set aside.

Beat the egg whites until they hold soft peaks. Stir some of this into the sauce, to make it easier to work in the remainder, then stir in the rest of the egg whites. Pour into the soufflé dish and set it in a pan of hot water. Put it in the oven and turn the heat down to 375°. Bake for 35 to 40 minutes, until the top is well puffed and nicely browned.

Serves 4

ASPARAGUS SOUFFLÉ

3	tablespoons melted butter	4	eggs, separated
3	tablespoons flour	2¹/₂	cups diced cooked asparagus
1	cup milk	¹/₂ to 1	teaspoon salt
¹/₃	cup heavy cream		

*B*lend the butter and flour, add the milk and cream gradually, and cook until thick, stirring constantly. Beat the egg yolks until lemon-colored and thick. Add the yolks, asparagus, and salt to the white sauce, mix, and remove from the heat. Beat the egg whites until very stiff and fold into the other ingredients. Pour into a buttered 1¹/₂- to 2-quart soufflé dish and set it in a pan of hot water. Bake in a preheated 400° oven for about 20 minutes.
Serves 4

GRAND MARNIER SOUFFLÉ

2	tablespoons butter, softened	¹/₄	cup Grand Marnier
¹/₃	cup plus 3 tablespoons sugar	1	tablespoon freshly grated orange zest
5	eggs, separated, plus 2 egg whites	¹/₄	tablespoon cream of tartar

Grand Marnier Sauce

1¹/₂	cups sugar		Large pinch of cream of tartar
¹/₂	cup water		
		1	jigger Grand Marnier

*P*reheat the oven to 450°. Grease a 1¹/₂- to 2-quart soufflé dish with the softened butter and sprinkle with the 3 tablespoons sugar. Discard any excess.

In a double boiler set over simmering water, beat the egg yolks until well blended. Slowly add the remaining sugar, and continue beating until the yolks are thick and pale yellow. Stir in the Grand Marnier and orange zest and set it over ice until quite cold, stirring occasionally with a wooden spoon.

Beat the egg whites and cream of tartar until stiff. Mix a few spoonfuls with the egg yolk mixture, then fold in the rest. Spoon into the soufflé dish to within 2 inches of the top. Smooth the top with a rubber spatula, then make a cap on the top by cutting a trench 1 inch deep 1 inch in from the edge of the dish. Set the dish in a pan of hot water and bake on the middle shelf of the oven for 2 minutes or so, then reduce the heat to 400°. Bake for another 25 to 30 minutes, until the soufflé has risen about 2 inches above the top of the dish.

Meanwhile, make the sauce. Cook 1 cup sugar with the water and cream of tartar. In a small saucepan, cook the remaining 1/2 cup sugar until it is caramelized. Add it to the mixture, along with the Grand Marnier. Serve hot with the soufflé.

Serves 4

Variation: Instead of the sauce, top the soufflé with powdered sugar.

CRÊPES

1/2	cup sifted flour	1	tablespoon melted
1	large egg		butter
1 1/4	cups milk		

*M*ix all of the ingredients in a food processor or blender. Let it relax for at least an hour before making the crêpes. The pancakes must be very thin, so use just enough butter in the skillet to prevent sticking. Pour in just enough batter to form a film, and cook gently on each side. Stack between sheets of wax paper, let cool, and refrigerate or freeze until ready to use.

To serve, melt a little butter in a pan and briefly heat the crêpes. Fill with anything you like—for a sweet crêpe, fruit; wine or liqueur; or sugar and citrus zest—and fold in quarters.

Makes 16

BAKING

Breads and Rolls

*B*aking is easy, but it is not simple. I will give two examples of how to make something neat and spiffy—the infamous dinner roll and the even more infamous French bread.

Breads and rolls can be brushed with various glazes before being baked. Each gives a different crust. Egg white mixed with water produces a dark, shiny crust. Plain water makes it softer and not quite as dark. Egg yolk makes it heavier and tastier. Milk results in a frosted glaze. Butter makes the top flaky and crackly.

GREAT DINNER ROLLS

2 packages dry yeast	1/2 teaspoon salt
1 cup lukewarm milk (100°)	4 cups sifted white bread flour
1/4 teaspoon sugar	1 egg, beaten

*D*issolve the yeast in the warm milk. Add the sugar and salt and half of the flour. Beat in the egg with a wooden spoon. Add the rest of the flour and beat again. Cover with a damp kitchen towel and let it rise in the refrigerator overnight, or until doubled in bulk. Punch the dough down, and all you have to do after that is take small pieces of dough, shape them into small or medium-size rolls, and set them in a baking pan. Let them rise in a warm (75° to 80°), draft-free place (such as an unlighted oven) for 25 minutes. Brush the tops with egg yolk, milk, or melted butter to glaze them. Bake in a preheated 400° oven for 12 to 15 minutes, until golden brown.

Makes 18 to 24

Note: Test baked yeast goods for doneness with a toothpick, inserted in the thickest part. If it comes out clean, not wet or sticky, the baking is done. A good test for bread is to tap the loaf on the bottom; if it sounds hollow, it is done.

Try this recipe and really enjoy being able to serve fresh, hot dinner rolls anytime, with the dough ready and waiting in the refrigerator.

FRENCH BREAD

Small pinch of sugar	4 cups sifted white bread flour
1 1/4 cups warm water (110°)	2 teaspoons salt
1 1/2 packages dry yeast	

*S*tir the sugar into the warm water and sprinkle in the yeast. Let stand for 5 minutes or so, until the surface becomes frothy. Stir gently to mix in any dry particles. Sift the flour and salt into a large mixing bowl, pour in the yeast liquid, and mix to make a dough. Flour a board or counter and knead the dough on it for 5 to 10 minutes, until it becomes smooth and elastic. Sprinkle the dough with flour, to prevent it from forming a crust, cover with a damp kitchen towel, and let it rise at room temperature for 2 to 3 hours.

Knead the risen dough very quickly. Divide into 2 pieces and shape them into long rolls. Place them on floured baking sheet pans, cover the dough, and let stand in a warm, draft-free place for 30 minutes.

Slash the loaves diagonally several times with a sharp knife and brush with lukewarm water. Bake in a preheated 425° oven for 15 minutes, then reduce the heat to 350° and bake for 15 to 20 minutes, until the loaves are golden brown and crusty.

Makes 2 loaves

WHITE BREAD

9 to 10 cups sifted flour	1 quart heated
1/4 cup sugar	milk (100°)
1 teaspoon salt	1 large egg
2 envelopes dry yeast	

*I*n an electric mixer, mix 3 cups flour with the sugar, salt, and yeast. Add the milk slowly and beat for 2 minutes at medium speed. Add the egg and 2 cups flour and beat for 2 minutes at high speed. Add the rest of the flour and knead for 8 to 10 minutes. Put in an oiled bowl, turn the dough to oil it on all sides, cover, and let rise in a warm, draft-free place until doubled in bulk. Punch down. Let rise again at 80° for 45 minutes. Bake in a preheated 400° oven for 15 to 20 minutes, until brown.

Makes 2 loaves

ANOTHER WHITE BREAD

1 cup warm water (110°)	1 cup milk, scalded and
Small pinch of ginger	cooled
2 tablespoons sugar	About 4 cups sifted
1 package dry yeast	flour (depending on
2 teaspoons salt	the amount of
2 tablespoons butter	moisture in the flour)
	Olive oil

*M*ix the water, ginger, sugar, and yeast. Let sit until the yeast activates, 4 to 5 minutes. Add the salt, butter, and milk, stir, and start adding flour, about 2 cups in the beginning. Keep adding flour until it forms a sticky but cohesive dough. Add flour as required while kneading to get a satiny-smooth and soft dough. Roll it into a ball and lightly coat with olive oil. Cover it and let rise in a warm, draft-free place until doubled in bulk.

Punch it down and let rise again. Punch it down and let it sit for 10 minutes, then form into 2 loaves (or into rolls or buns or whatever). Again lightly coat with olive oil and let rise, set in pans or on sheets or whatever. Bake rolls or buns in a preheated 400° oven for 20 to 25 minutes. Bake bread at 400° for 15 minutes or more, until somewhat crusty and resistant, then turn the oven down to 375° and continue baking for 1 hour or more, until done. You can brush the tops with water, egg white, or butter during the baking, depending on the glaze you are looking to achieve.

Makes 2 loaves or 24 rolls or buns

SOURDOUGH STARTER

About 4 large potatoes	2 tablespoons sugar
2 cups sifted flour	1/2 teaspoon dry yeast

*B*oil the potatoes in their jackets until they fall to pieces. It may take even more than 4 potatoes, if they are old. Remove the potato skins and purée the potatoes and liquid. Let cool. Measure out the volume; if necessary, add water to make 2 cups. Add the remaining ingredients and beat until creamy.

Cover and set aside in a warm place to ferment. Use only after a week has gone by.

Keep the starter refrigerated. Replenish it as you use it up— use half or at most three quarters of it, cook up another batch, let it ferment, and replace the amount that you removed.

What to do with it? Try the following recipe.

Thanks to Mary, the owner of the Black Castle Lodge near Delta Junction, Alaska, I am in possession of one of the best sourdough starter recipes I have ever seen or used.

Don't even begin to think that all of the recipes in this book are mine, for they are not, and I am indebted to some great chefs and cooks from my past for such gifts.

FRENCH BREAD SOURDOUGH STYLE

1	cup sourdough starter	6	cups flour
2	tablespoons sugar	1	tablespoon salt
1½	cups warm water (110°)	½	teaspoon baking soda

*M*ix the starter, sugar, water, and 3 cups flour in a large plastic bowl. Cover it with plastic wrap or a kitchen towel and let it stand at room temperature for at least 12 hours.

Combine the salt, soda, and 1 cup flour. Beat until it becomes smooth, adding enough of the remaining flour to make the dough soft. Turn it out onto a floured board and mix in enough of the remaining flour to make it stiff enough to knead. Knead for at least 10 minutes, then stretch and roll it into a French-style loaf. Put it on a greased cookie sheet, cover, and let rise in a warm, draft-free place for at least 2 hours, or until doubled in bulk. Slash the top of the loaf at an angle four or five times, then brush it with butter, milk, or water. Bake in a preheated 375° oven for 30 minutes, or until done.

Makes 1 loaf

POTATO RYE

2	tablespoons dry yeast	1	cup firmly packed hot mashed potatoes
1	tablespoon sea salt		
1	tablespoon caraway seeds	4	cups whole-rye flour
2	cups hot (but not boiling) potato water (reserved from having cooked the potatoes)	2 to 2½	cups whole-wheat flour
			Melted butter
			Cornmeal

*I*n a large mixing bowl, combine the yeast, salt, caraway seeds, and potato water. Stir. Add the mashed potatoes and mix to distribute evenly. Stir in the rye flour, 2 cups at a time. Mix in 1 cup whole-wheat flour.

Spread 1 cup whole-wheat flour over a kneading board, scrape the batter onto the flour, and knead in the flour. Knead for 15 minutes after all of the flour is in; flour the board as required to handle the dough (up to ½ cup whole-wheat flour may be called for). If, after 15 minutes, you are not feeling resistance when you knead, knead for another 5 or 10 minutes. Form the dough into a ball and put it in an oiled mixing bowl. Turn the dough to oil it on all sides and let it rise, covered by a hot, wet kitchen towel, in a warm, draft-free place for 1½ to 2 hours, until doubled in bulk.

Punch the dough down and knead out any large air bubbles. Cut the dough in half and knead each half into a smooth ball. Shape them into loaves about 8 × 4 inches. Brush a cookie sheet with melted butter and sprinkle with cornmeal. Set the loaves on the cookie sheet and, with a sharp or serrated knife, slash each loaf diagonally in three or four diagonal places, about ½ inch deep. Cover with a dry kitchen towel and let them rise again for 30 minutes to an hour.

Remove the towel and brush the loaves with water. Bake them in a preheated 375° oven for 15 minutes; brush again (or spray) with water and bake for another 35 minutes. Turn off the heat and let the loaves sit in the oven for 10 minutes. Rap the bottom crust for the hollow sound that indicates doneness. Let cool on a wire rack for half an hour.

Makes 2 loaves

Variation: Substituting all or part rye meal for the rye flour makes the bread chewier.

Rye breads call for a lot of kneading—at least 15 minutes. If you get tired partway, cover the dough with an inverted bowl and take a break.

SWEDISH RYE

2 tablespoons fennel seeds	1 teaspoon sea salt
2 tablespoons dry yeast	Grated zest of 1 orange
1/4 cup blackstrap molasses	1/4 cup vegetable oil
1/4 cup honey	3 cups whole-rye flour
2 cups hot (but not boiling) potato water (from having cooked potatoes)	31/2 to 4 cups whole-wheat flour
	Melted butter
	Cornmeal
	Milk

*W*ith a mortar and pestle, or the back of a spoon against the mixing bowl, coarsely crush the fennel seeds. Add the yeast, molasses, honey, and potato water. Stir to mix. Add the salt, zest, and oil. Stir. Thoroughly mix in the rye flour, then 3 cups whole-wheat flour.

Spread 1/2 cup whole-wheat flour over the kneading board and scrape the batter onto the flour. Knead in. Knead for 15 minutes, using as much of the remaining 1/2 cup flour as necessary. Oil a mixing bowl, shape the dough into a ball, and turn it in the bowl to oil it on all sides. Cover with a hot, wet kitchen towel and set in a warm, draft-free place to rise for about 11/2 hours, until doubled in bulk.

Punch the dough down and knead it to eliminate large air

bubbles. Cut the dough into 3 pieces and roll them into 3 smooth balls. Roll each out into a loaf about 2 × 14 inches. Brush 2 cookie sheets with melted butter and sprinkle with a thin layer of cornmeal. Set the loaves on the sheets, prick the tops all over with a fork, cover with a dry towel, and let them rise again for 30 to 45 minutes.

With a light hand, brush the tops with milk, and bake in a preheated 375° oven for about 30 minutes. Rap the bottom to test for doneness and let cool on a wire rack for a few minutes. Serve hot.

Makes 3 loaves

Variations: Replace half or all of the potato water with beer, and increase the salt by 1 teaspoon.

For a hard crust, brush the bread twice with water (as for potato rye) instead of using milk.

Brushing the top with milk gives this bread a soft crust.

REFRIGERATOR RYE

2 tablespoons dry yeast	2 cups hot water
1 tablespoon sea salt	3 cups whole-rye flour
1/3 cup blackstrap molasses	3 to 31/2 cups sifted white flour
1/4 cup vegetable oil	Melted butter

*I*n a mixing bowl, combine the yeast, salt, molasses, oil, and hot water. Stir. Mix in the rye flour, then 2 cups white flour.

Spread 1 cup white flour over the kneading board and scrape the dough out onto it. Knead it, adding only as much of the remaining 1/2 cup white flour as necessary to keep the dough from sticking. When the dough stops sticking, knead for another 10 minutes. It will be cohesive and get quite springy as it approaches readiness. Divide it into 3 parts and shape each into a loaf to fit an 8 × 4 × 2-inch loaf pan. Brush the pans with melted butter and put a loaf in each. With your fingers, level the top of each loaf. Cover each pan with greased plastic wrap. Don't make the plastic taut and don't try to fasten it to the sides; it will rise with the dough. Set the pans in the refrigerator and let the loaves rise there for 5 to 24 hours.

Carefully remove the plastic wrap, and bake immediately in a preheated 375° oven for about 45 minutes. Test for doneness and let cool on a wire rack.

Makes 3 loaves

Variation: Add 1 tablespoon caraway, fennel, or anise seeds to the mixing bowl, or knead them in when shaping the loaves.

PUMPERNICKEL

3	tablespoons dry yeast	1/4	cup vegetable oil
2	teaspoons sea salt	2	cups whole-rye flour
1/4	cup blackstrap molasses	2	cups whole-wheat flour
1	tablespoon Postum or instant coffee powder	1 to 2	cups sifted white flour
2	cups hot water		Melted butter
			White cornmeal

Glaze

1   teaspoon Postum or instant coffee
    dissolved in 2 teaspoons water

*I*n a large mixing bowl, combine the yeast, salt, molasses, Postum, and hot water. Stir. Mix in the oil. Mix in the rye flour, then the whole-wheat flour.

Spread 1 cup white flour over the kneading board, scrape the batter out onto the board, and knead for 15 minutes, adding as much of the remaining white flour as necessary to keep the dough from sticking. Oil a mixing bowl, shape the dough into a ball, and turn it in the bowl to oil it on all sides. Cover with a hot, wet kitchen towel and set in a warm, draft-free place to rise, about 1 to 1 1/2 hours.

Punch the dough down, knead it briefly to eliminate large air bubbles, and cut it into 3 pieces. Shape them into round or oval loaves. Brush 2 large cookie sheets with melted butter and sprinkle with cornmeal. Set the loaves on the sheets, cover with a dry towel, and let them rise for 30 to 45 minutes.

Gently brush the tops with the glaze. Bake in a preheated 375° oven for 50 minutes to 1 hour. If the loaves look close to scorching after 50 minutes, but still seem raw, shut the oven off for the last 10 minutes of baking. Let cool on a wire rack and eat warm.

Makes 3 loaves

CROISSANTS

4 cups (1 pound) plus 5 tablespoons (or as needed) sifted flour, plus extra flour for dusting	1 1/2 packages dry yeast or 2/3 ounce fresh yeast
5 tablespoons sugar	2 1/2 sticks (1 1/4 cups) unsalted butter, cold
1 1/2 teaspoons salt	1 egg, lightly beaten with 2 tablespoons milk
1 1/2 cups milk	

Combine the 4 cups flour, sugar, and salt in a large mixing bowl and stir with a wooden spoon to mix.

Heat the milk in a small heavy saucepan to about 100°, or mildly warm to the touch. Sprinkle dry yeast over the milk and let stand until the milk has soaked through all of the yeast particles (or crumble in the fresh yeast and let stand until dissolved). Whisk until thoroughly blended (feel the bottom and sides of the pan for lumps). Pour the mixture into the dry ingredients. With a wooden spoon, stir the dry mixture from the sides of the bowl into the center. When no dry flour or clumps of dampened flour can be seen, beat with the spoon for 30 seconds, until the dough is somewhat smoother but loose and sticky. Do not overwork it. Cover with plastic wrap and refrigerate for 8 hours or overnight. The dough will double in bulk and become very light and spongy.

The next day, sprinkle the 5 ounces of flour on a work surface. Cut the butter into thin slices lengthwise and press both sides in the flour; work quickly to keep the butter hard and cool. Press it all together to form a long loaf of butter with flour throughout. Refrigerate it for about an hour.

Remove the dough to the work surface. It will be too spongy and fragile to roll out, so use your hands to flatten it and stretch it out to about 8 × 14 inches. Lightly mark the dough into 3 sections. Take out the butter and break off small egg-size lumps. Press them flat, lay them over two thirds of the dough (keep a 1-inch border at the sides unbuttered), and fold the other section over it. Press the ends of the dough together to seal, using the palms of your hands, but don't flatten them too thin.

Dust the work surface with flour, lay the dough down on it gently, and gently work it with your hands to incorporate the butter throughout the layers of dough. With a rolling pin, gently press the dough down in ridges. Every so often, lift the dough to check that it does not stick to the work surface. Roll the dough out to about 10 × 24, then fold it into thirds, as in the previous paragraph. This completes the first turn. Always keeping the folded crease to your right, roll it out again to about 10 × 24 inches and about 1/4 inch thick. When you have done this twice (three turns in all), fold it again into thirds, wrap with plastic wrap, cover with a damp kitchen towel, and refrigerate for about 20 hours.

Flour the work surface and put the dough on it. Let it warm up for about 5 minutes. If necessary, you can gently warm it by pressing lightly with your palms; your body heat lets the buttered layers soften enough to be workable. Begin to work the dough, rolling it out with a rolling pin; be careful not to roll the very ends too thin. When it is about 9 × 18 inches, roll it out lengthwise and widthwise to about 10 × 24 inches. Fold it over into 3 layers and repeat (the dough has been turned a total of five times). Refrigerate the folded dough for about 2 hours; the total refrigeration time should come to no more than 24 hours.

To make croissants, flour the work surface and let it rest for about 5 minutes. Roll the dough out to about 18 × 21 inches and 1/4 inch thick. If you have a pastry wheel, use it to cut and trim the edges of the dough (reserve the trimmings) and also to cut the shape of the croissants, which is a triangle. Cut them evenly and put a piece of dough from the reserved trimmings in the centers, to make the croissants flakier. Roll them up, starting with the base of the triangle. Shape them into horseshoe forms, set on cookie sheets, and brush with the egg wash; do not let it drip on the cookie sheets. Let them rise until doubled in bulk, which could take from 45 minutes to 2¹/2 hours, depending on the warmth of the room.

Heat the oven to 375° and bake the croissants until a medium dark brown, about 25 minutes. The color should be uniform and there should be no white streaks along the creases.

Makes 18 to 20

Variations: Filled croissants. Mix diced ham and Dijon mustard, and perhaps some cheese. Fill the croissants, roll up, and bake. For a sweet filling, mix 1/3 cup blanched almonds, 1/2 cup sugar, 1/4 teaspoon cinnamon, and 1 egg white. Put about 1 tablespoon in each croissant, roll up, let rise, and bake.

Chocolate-Filled Croissants. Chop up semisweet chocolate into pieces the size of small peas. Cut the croissant dough into squares and put pieces of chocolate in each, just a bit off center. Brush the edges with egg wash, fold it in thirds, brush the top with melted butter, and bake.

MY FAVORITE CROISSANT

3³/4 cups sifted flour	Pinch of salt
2/3 to 1 ounce dry yeast	1¹/2 sticks (³/4 cup)
1 cup lukewarm milk (100°)	butter, softened

*S*ift the flour onto a board, make a well in the center, put the yeast in the well, and moisten it with a bit of milk. Mix in one quarter of the flour and let rise. Add the salt, butter, and remaining milk, and mix in all of the flour, moistening with additional milk if necessary. The dough should be firm, though, rather than soft. Roll it into a ball, cover with a damp cloth, and let rise in a warm, draft-free place.

Divide the dough into pieces about the size of an egg. Roll them out into ovals with a floured rolling pin. (If you prefer, roll out the dough in large sheets and cut them into triangles.) Roll up each piece and curve it into a crescent. Place them on a cookie sheet, let them rise, and brush with a little extra milk. Bake in a hot preheated 375° oven for 8 to 12 minutes, until golden brown. When you remove them from the oven, brush them very lightly with melted butter.

Makes 18 to 20

PIZZA

1/2	envelope dry yeast	2	teaspoons salt
1/3	cup warm water (110°)	4	tablespoons butter
1 1/2	cups sifted flour	1	egg, beaten

Suggested Toppings

	Spaghetti sauce (page 126)		Oregano
1	pound mozzarella cheese, sliced	1	green pepper, seeded and sliced
1	pepperoni, sliced		Black olives, sliced
4 to 5	mushrooms, sliced and sautéed		Pepper

Soften the yeast in the water. Sift the flour and 1 teaspoon salt into a bowl. Work in the butter with your fingers. Add the egg to the yeast, then stir into the flour mixture until a ball of dough is formed. If it is too stiff, add a little more water. Knead on a lightly floured surface until smooth and elastic. Form into a ball, place in an oiled bowl, turn to oil the dough on all sides, cover with a towel, and let rise in a warm place for 2 hours. Divide the dough in half and roll out for 2 8-inch pizzas.

Spread spaghetti sauce on the dough and top with whatever

you like, in amounts to your taste. Bake in a preheated 400°
oven for 10 to 12 minutes, watching that it doesn't burn on top.
Makes 2 8-inch pizzas

STICKY BUNS

1	package dry yeast	1	teaspoon grated lemon zest
1/2	cup warm water (110°)	1	teaspoon cinnamon
1/2	cup plus 1 pinch sugar	1/2	cup currants or raisins
1	cup milk	1 1/2	cups firmly packed brown sugar
8	tablespoons melted butter (1 stick)	4	tablespoons butter
3 1/2	cups sifted flour	1/2	cup coarsely chopped walnuts
1/4	teaspoon salt		
2	egg yolks		

*S*prinkle the yeast into the warm water, along with the pinch
of sugar. Let stand for 2 to 3 minutes, then stir to dissolve the
yeast. Set in warm, draft-free place for 5 to 8 minutes, or until
it has begun to bubble and is almost doubled in volume.

Pour the milk into a heavy 1-quart saucepan and warm it
over medium heat until bubbles form around the edges of the
pan. Turn the heat to low and add 4 tablespoons melted butter
and 1/4 cup of the sugar. Stir until the sugar dissolves, then let
cool to lukewarm and add the yeast mixture.

Sift the flour and salt into a deep mixing bowl. Make a well
and pour into it the yeast mixture, egg yolks, and lemon zest.
With your hands or a wooden spoon, work the flour into the
other ingredients until it forms a medium-firm dough. On a
lightly floured surface, knead the dough by folding it end to
end, then pressing it down and pushing forward several times
with the heel of your hand. Sprinkle the dough with a little
extra flour whenever necessary to keep it from sticking to the
board. Knead until the dough becomes smooth and elastic,
about 10 minutes. Shape the dough into a ball and put it in a
buttered large bowl. Dust the top with just a bit of flour, cover

with a kitchen towel, and set in a warm place. It should double in about an hour.

Punch the dough down, then knead it briefly on a lightly floured board. Roll it out into a rectangle 12 inches long and 1/4 inch thick. Brush with 3 tablespoons melted butter. Combine the remaining 1/4 cup sugar with the cinnamon and currants, and sprinkle evenly over the dough.

In a small heavy saucepan, combine the brown sugar and 4 tablespoons butter with 1/2 cup water. Stir until the sugar dissolves; bring to a boil over high heat. Reduce the heat to moderate and cook the syrup for about 10 minutes, until it has the consistency and color of maple syrup. Let the syrup cool slightly, then drizzle half of it over the dough. Roll the dough into a tight cylinder about 2 inches in diameter, and cut it crosswise into 1-inch rounds.

Grease a 10-inch round cake pan with the remaining 1 teaspoon melted butter, pour in the remaining syrup, and sprinkle evenly with the chopped nuts. Arrange the rounds, on their side, in a circle around the edge of the pan; continue the pattern with the remaining rounds until the pan is full. Let them rise in a warm, draft-free place for about 25 minutes, until doubled in bulk. Heat the oven to 350° and bake the buns in the middle of the oven for about 30 minutes. When the buns are golden brown and firm to the touch, remove them from the oven and invert onto a cake rack. Separate and serve.

Makes 1 dozen

MUFFINS

2 cups sifted flour	1/4 cup butter or margarine, softened
3 teaspoons baking powder	1 cup milk
1/2 teaspoon salt	1 egg
1/4 cup sugar	

Sift all of the dry ingredients into a mixing bowl. Mix well. Add the butter, milk, and egg. Mix just to blend; do not overmix. Butter a muffin tin, fill the cups about two thirds full, and bake in a preheated 400° oven for 25 to 30 minutes.

Makes 1 dozen

Variations: Whole Wheat Muffins. Substitute 1 cup whole wheat flour for 1 of the cups all-purpose flour and reduce the baking powder from 3 teaspoons to 2.

Sour Milk Muffins. Substitute 1 cup sour milk for regular milk and use only 2 teaspoons baking powder plus 1/2 teaspoon baking soda.

Most people love muffins, but few realize how simple they are to make.

SWEET MUFFINS

1 1/2	cups sifted flour	1/2	cup milk
2	teaspoons baking powder	1/2	cup sugar
1/4	cup shortening or butter, softened	1/2	teaspoon salt
		1	egg

*P*repare as in the previous recipe.
Makes 1 dozen

Variations: Apple Muffins. Add 1 teaspoon cinnamon and 1 cup chopped apple with the liquid ingredients. Bake for 30 minutes, or until done.

Blueberry Muffins. Add 1 cup fresh blueberries or 3/4 cup drained canned or thawed frozen blueberries.

BAKING POWDER BISCUITS

2	cups sifted flour	1/2	teaspoon salt
1	teaspoon sugar	4	tablespoons butter or shortening
3	teaspoons baking powder	3/4	cup milk

*S*ift the dry ingredients into a bowl, then work in the butter until it is evenly mixed and crumbly. Add the milk all at once, stirring only until the dough is puffy soft. Scoop out the dough onto a lightly floured pastry cloth. Flour your hands, pat the dough into a thick square, then squeeze it together. Knead 5 or 6 times so the biscuits will rise evenly. Pat out the dough to a square 1 inch thick. Dip a 2-inch cutter in flour and cut out the biscuits, working from the outside in, so there will be very few scraps to reroll. Set the rounds 1 inch apart on a greased cookie sheet and bake in a preheated 425° oven for about 12 minutes, until golden brown.

Makes 10 to 12

POPOVERS

1 cup sifted flour	1 cup milk
2 eggs	1/2 teaspoon salt

*H*eat the oven to 425°. In an electric mixer, beat all of the ingredients until very smooth. Butter large muffin tins or large timbale cups and put them in the oven until smoking hot. Fill them three quarters full of batter. Bake for 35 to 40 minutes, until crisp and golden brown. Don't open the oven door to look at them. If you have a glass door, fine; if not, wait the prescribed time before opening the door.

Makes about 8

SESAME WAFERS

8 tablespoons (1 stick) butter, softened	2 large pinches baking powder
1 1/2 cups light brown sugar	1 teaspoon vanilla extract
1 egg	1 cup toasted sesame seeds
4 cups flour	

*I*n a mixing bowl, cream the butter, sugar, and egg. Mix the flour and baking powder and stir in. Beat well. Add the vanilla extract and sesame seeds and beat to mix well. Put about 1 teaspoon per wafer on greased cookie sheets and bake in a preheated 350° oven for 9 to 10 minutes. Let cool somewhat on the cookie sheets, then set them on racks to finish cooling.

Makes 9 dozen

Pastry

PUFF PASTRY

5	cups sifted flour	2 1/4	cups cold water
11	sticks (5 1/2 cups, 2 3/4 pounds) butter	1/2	teaspoon salt
		3	small or 2 large eggs

*I*n an electric mixer, mix the flour, 1 stick butter, water, salt, and egg. Take the dough out of the mixer and roll it into a ball, then let the dough stand for about 20 minutes.

Lay the dough on a floured work surface and roll it out to a 14- to 16-inch square, leaving the center of the dough a bit thicker than the edges. Put the remaining 10 sticks butter in the center of the dough. Fold the corners of the square into the center, overlapping one another. Flatten out with a rolling pin, then roll out to form a rectangle about 1/2 inch thick. Brush off any excess flour and fold the dough into thirds, as you would fold a business letter to fit into an envelope, first one side over, then the other. Refrigerate for half an hour.

Take it out, roll it out and fold it again, and put it back in the refrigerator. Repeat this procedure at least four times.

After the last chilling, cut it to the size you need. Bake in a preheated 375° oven for 25 to 30 minutes, until it is nice and crisp.

Makes about 50 squares

Note: The dough can be kept refrigerated or frozen, but you must always roll it out again and let it come to room temperature (about half an hour) before cutting and baking it.

Puff Pastry Desserts: Napoleons. Roll out the puff pastry very thin and bake on a cookie sheet. Take it out and cut the pastry into 3 pieces. Spread the first piece with a soft custard (page 223), top with another layer, fill again, top again, and then top this with a vanilla frosting. Streak with lines of melted chocolate, and draw a knife across the frosting to make the characteristic design.

Cream Slices. Make napoleons and fill with a flavored whipped cream or Bavarian cream (page 224).

Nut Pastry. Roll out the dough, butter it slightly, sprinkle crushed almonds, pecans, or walnuts on it. Cut into pieces about 2 × 4 inches and bake as above. Take them out, cut in half, and fill with anything you like.

Apple Turnovers. Brush pastry dough squares with water, fill with apples (cooked with sugar, lemon juice, and cinnamon) in the center, fold into a triangle, brush with water or egg wash, and bake.

With this pastry dough you can make so many different desserts that you will never be at a loss as to what to serve guests. You must follow the formula exactly for it to come out right. (Or see the next recipe.)

EASY PUFF PASTRY

1/2	cup water	1/4	teaspoon salt
4	tablespoons butter	2	eggs
1/2	cup sifted flour		

*P*ut the water in a pan, bring to a boil, and add the butter; cook, stirring until melted. Mix together the flour and salt and stir it in with a wooden spoon over low heat. When it begins to pull away from the pan it is ready. Remove it from the heat and add the eggs, one at a time, beating vigorously after each addition. Put the mixture in a pastry tube and pipe it onto a greased cookie sheet. Bake in a preheated 450° oven for 5 minutes, then at 375° for 40 minutes. *Never open the oven door while baking this type of pastry.*

Makes 6 tart shells or 2 pie crusts

ÉCLAIRS OR CREAM PUFFS

Pâte à Choux

1 cup water	Pinch of salt
4 tablespoons butter	4 eggs, beaten
1 cup sifted all-purpose or bread flour	

Filling

2 cups heavy cream	1 teaspoon instant coffee
1/2 cup sugar	

*H*eat the water and butter to a boil. Add the flour and salt all at once. Stirring with a wooden spoon, cook over low heat until the mixture becomes very smooth and rolls away from the sides of the pan. Take it off the heat, transfer to a large bowl, and let cool slightly. Add the eggs, one at a time, beating well after each addition. Use to fill a pastry bag with a fluted nozzle and squeeze out hot-dog shapes, éclairs, or round shapes, for cream puffs. Bake on a buttered cookie sheet in a preheated 400° oven for 30 minutes. *Do not open the oven at any time during the baking.*

Whip the cream to the soft-peaks stage, then begin whipping in the sugar and coffee powder. Pipe into the cooled pastry—from the end for éclairs, from the side for cream puffs.

Makes about 1 dozen

Variation: Instead of instant coffee, use coffee extract or vanilla extract.

PIE CRUST

2 cups (1 pound) sifted
    pastry flour
	1 1/4 cups lard or
	       shortening

1/4 teaspoon salt	6 ounces plus ice water

*M*ix the flour and salt in a mixing bowl, add the lard, and rub together to the size of walnuts, for a flaky crust, or small peas, for mealy crust. Begin adding the ice water. Mix the dough with your hands until it just comes together, but *do not overwork it.* Once it has reached a form of dough, stop; just roll it together, put it on a floured board, and roll it out gently. The less you handle it the flakier it will be.

You can use this crust for any type of pie. You can top any pie with the same crust, or make an open type. If you make an open pie, first partially bake the crust in a preheated 400° oven for 8 to 12 minutes, weighted with dried beans or marbles. This cooking ensures that the crust will not be too mealy on the bottom. The total baking time for exposed pie crust should come to no more than 24 to 30 minutes. If a filling recipe calls for more time than that, wrap the exposed crust with foil to keep it from burning.

Makes 1 double-crust pie or 2 bottom-crust pies

Variation: Quick Sweet Pastry Dough. Use butter rather than lard or shortening, mix with the flour and salt, plus 1/4 cup sugar, and add a package of dry yeast dissolved in a bit of lukewarm water; let it set for a few minutes before adding the ice water. Roll out and cut into the desired shape.

FLAN PASTRY

2¹/2	cups sifted flour	¹/3	cup sugar
	Small pinch of salt	1	egg
14	tablespoons (7 ounces) butter		

*S*ift the flour and salt into a mixing bowl and, using a fork or knife, mix in the butter evenly. Mix in the sugar and egg and make into a dough. Wrap it up and refrigerate for at least 1 to 3 hours. When you are ready to use it, roll it out, place it in an 11- to 12-inch flan pan, and bake as for pie crust, weighted with dried beans or marbles. Fill it with a custard. Depending on the filling, make a lattice topping or, as is more usual, leave the top open.

Makes 1 11- to 12-inch flan

Variations: You can make any type of fruit flan by proceeding as for a fruit pie; or just make a bottom glaze for the baked pastry, place cooked fruit on it, and top with another glaze or a cooked mixed fruit topping. For example, put a coating of cream cheese on the pastry and place fresh blueberries or strawberries on it; cook 1 to 2 cups berries with sugar and a bit of brandy, thicken with a bit of arrowroot powder mixed with a bit of water, and pour over the fresh berries. Bake in a preheated 375° oven for 35 to 40 minutes. Take it out and let cool on a rack. Top with powdered sugar or whipped cream.

APPLE STRUDEL

Pastry

1/2	cup warm water	1	tablespoon sugar
2	tablespoons plus vegetable oil	2	cups sifted flour
		1	egg plus 1 egg white

8	tart green apples		Freshly grated cinnamon, nutmeg, and lemon zest
2	tablespoons lemon juice		
	Melted butter	1/2	cup ground toasted almonds
1/4	cup granulated sugar		
1/4	cup firmly packed light brown sugar		Powdered sugar
			Whipped cream (optional)

*M*ake the pastry by blending the water, 2 tablespoons oil, and sugar in a small bowl. Mound the flour on a work surface, make a well in the center, and put the liquid mixture, egg, and egg white in the well. Gradually draw flour from the inner edge of the well into the center until all of the flour is incorporated. Gather the dough into a ball and slap it on the counter 100 times to develop the gluten. Rub the dough with oil, cover with an inverted bowl, and let stand for 30 minutes.

For the filling, peel, core, and thinly slice the apples. Sprinkle with lemon juice.

To assemble, oil a baking sheet pan and lightly oil your hands. Set the dough on a 48-inch round table covered with a tablecloth. Flatten the dough into a disk and press it into a large circle. Begin stretching the dough, pushing and pulling from the center outward, until it covers the entire table; it will be completely translucent. (Use floured cups to weight the edges.) Cut off and discard the thick edge of dough hanging over the table.

Heat the oven to 425°. Brush the dough with melted butter. Arrange the apple slices over three fourths of the dough and then sprinkle them with the sugars and dust with cinnamon, nutmeg, and lemon zest. Sprinkle the almonds over all of the dough. Using the tablecloth as an aid, roll the dough up into a log; tuck in the ends.

Set the strudel in the pan, formed into a U. Brush with melted butter. Bake for 15 minutes and brush again with butter. Reduce the oven temperature to 350° and bake for about 30 minutes, until golden brown. Let cool slightly in the pan. Cut into 2-inch pieces and sprinkle lightly with powdered sugar. Serve with either more powdered sugar over them or with whipped cream.

Serves 16

Cakes, Pies, and Tarts

CHOCOLATE MOUSSE CAKE

7	ounces semisweet chocolate	1	cup sugar
8	tablespoons (1 stick) unsalted butter	1	teaspoon vanilla extract
7	eggs, separated, at room temperature	1/8	teaspoon lemon juice

*H*eat the oven to 325°. Melt the chocolate and butter in a double boiler over simmering water. Stir until smooth. Whisk the yolks and 3/4 cup sugar until pale yellow and fluffy. Gradually stir in the chocolate and vanilla extract. Beat the whites with lemon juice until soft peaks form. Add the remaining sugar, 1 tablespoon at a time, and continue beating until stiff but not dry. Gently fold into the chocolate mixture. Pour three fourths of the batter into a buttered 9-inch springform pan; cover and refrigerate the remaining batter. Bake the cake for 35 minutes. Let cool completely. (The cake will fall as it cools, but don't let it bother you.) Trim the edges with a sharp knife and spread the remaining batter over the top. Refrigerate for at least 8 hours.

Makes 1 9-inch cake

BOURBON CHOCOLATE PECAN CAKE

12	ounces semisweet chocolate	3/4	cup sugar
2	sticks (1 cup) butter	1/2	cup bourbon
8	eggs, separated	1	pound ground pecans

Glaze

1	pound semisweet	Pecan halves
	chocolate, melted	
1/3	cup vegetable oil	

*I*n a double boiler over simmering water, mix and melt the chocolate and butter. Beat the egg yolks and sugar, and mix in the chocolate, a little at a time. Add the bourbon and mix. Beat the egg whites until stiff and fold them in, along with the pecans. Butter and sugar the bottom and sides of a 9-inch springform pan and, if you have some on hand, put baking paper on the bottom. Pour in the batter and bake in a preheated 300° oven for 1 1/2 to 1 3/4 hours. Let cool.

Mix the glaze, pour over the cake, and let set until firm. Garnish with pecan halves.

Makes 1 9-inch cake

LOUISIANA PECAN CAKE

1 1/2	packages seedless raisins, cut into halves	6	eggs, beaten
		4 1/2	cups sifted flour
1	cup whiskey	3 1/2	cups coarsely chopped pecans
2	sticks (1 cup) butter, softened	2	teaspoons baking powder
2 1/2	cups granulated sugar	1	teaspoon salt
1	nutmeg, grated		Confectioner's sugar

*S*oak the raisins in whiskey overnight; drain (you can drink the whiskey, which has fulfilled its purpose here). Cream the butter and granulated sugar. Add the nutmeg and eggs and beat thoroughly. Mix 1 cup of the flour with the nuts. Sift together the remaining flour, baking powder, and salt. Add the dry ingredients to the creamed mixture. Fold in the nuts, then the raisins. Mix lightly and pour into a well-buttered and well-floured 10-inch tube pan. Bake in a preheated 350° oven for 1 hour and 25 minutes, or until the cake tests done. Do not overbake. Let cool in the pan for 5 minutes, turn it out, and let cool on a cake rack. Sprinkle with confectioner's sugar.

Serves 6 to 8

FRUIT CAKE ROLL

2	tablespoons butter, softened		Pinch of salt
1/2	cup sifted flour, plus extra as needed	1/4	cup sugar
4	eggs, separated	1/2	teaspoon vanilla extract

Filling

11/2	cups heavy cream, chilled	1 to 2	teaspoons orange juice, or 1 cup marmalade or apricot preserves
4	tablespoons granulated sugar		
1	12-ounce can crushed pineapple, thoroughly drained		

3   tablespoons confectioner's sugar (optional)

*B*utter the bottom and sides of a 16 × 11-inch jelly roll pan. Line the pan with a strip of wax paper; let the extra paper extend over the edges. Use the remaining butter on the wax paper, and scatter a small handful of flour over it. Shake off the excess flour.

Heat the oven to 400°. In a mixing bowl, beat the egg whites and salt until they form soft peaks. Add the sugar, 2 tablespoons at a time, and beat until the whites cling solidly to the lifted beater. In another small bowl, beat egg yolks for about a

minute, then add the vanilla extract. Mix in a large tablespoonful of the whites, then pour it over the egg whites. Fold together, adding the 1/2 cup flour, 2 tablespoons at a time.

Pour the batter into the jelly roll pan and spread it out
evenly. Bake for about 12 minutes, until the cake draws slightly
away from the sides of the pan, and a small knife inserted in the
center comes out dry and clean. Turn it out on a double thickness of wax paper about 22 inches long. Remove the wax paper
lining from the top of the cake and let cool to room temperature.

Beat the cream until slightly thickened, then pour in the
granulated sugar and continue to beat to the stiff-peaks stage.
With a rubber spatula, fold it into the pineapple and juice or
marmalade. Spread the mixture evenly over the cake. Roll it up
as you would a jelly roll and serve as is or chilled. If you used
the orange juice, shake confectioner's sugar over the roll.

Serves 8

FRESH PEACH COBBLER

1 1/2	cups sugar	6	cups sliced peeled peaches
2	tablespoons cornstarch	3	teaspoons butter
2	cups boiling water	1	teaspoon cinnamon

Shortcake

6	tablespoons shortening	3	teaspoons baking powder
2	cups sifted flour		
2/3	cup milk	2	tablespoons sugar

*M*ix the sugar and cornstarch and stir in the boiling water.
Bring to a boil and continue boiling for 1 minute. Add the
fruit. Pour into a baking dish, dot with butter, and sprinkle
with cinnamon.

Sift together the dry ingredients and rub in the shortening
with your hands until little beads form. Stir in the milk. Roll

out on a floured board until 1/2 inch thick. Cut into desired shapes with a cookie cutter.

Top the fruit with the shortcake dough. Bake in a preheated 400° oven for 30 minutes.

Serves 12

FRESH COCONUT CREAM PIE

1 cup sugar
1/2 cup cornstarch
1/4 teaspoon salt
3 cups hot milk
3 egg yolks, beaten
1 teaspoon vanilla extract
1/2 teaspoon almond extract

2 cups grated fresh coconut, or 2 31/2-ounce cans flaked coconut plus 1/2 cup sugar
1 baked 9-inch pie shell (page 185)
1 cup heavy cream

Combine the sugar, cornstarch, and salt in a saucepan. Add the milk and bring to a boil over medium heat, stirring constantly. Boil for 2 minutes and take off the heat. Stir half of the hot mixture into the egg yolks, then combine with the rest of it. Cook, stirring, over low heat until it boils and is thick enough to mound from the spoon, about 5 minutes. Turn into a bowl and stir in the extracts and half of the coconut. Place wax paper directly on the filling and refrigerate for 1 hour. Turn into the pie shell and refrigerate for 3 hours. Whip the cream and spread it over the pie. Top with the remaining coconut.

Makes 1 9-inch pie

CRANBERRY CREAM PIE

1 12-ounce package fresh cranberries
11/4 cups sugar
1 cup water
2 egg yolks, at room temperature

2 tablespoons cornstarch
1 cup sour cream, at room temperature
1 baked 9-inch pie shell (page 185)
Whipped cream

*C*ombine the cranberries, 1 cup sugar, and the water in a heavy saucepan. Cook over medium-high heat until very thick, about 10 minutes. Mix the yolks, remaining sugar, and cornstarch. Add to the cranberries, stir in the sour cream, and cook until thick, about 4 minutes. Spoon into the shell and refrigerate for at least 8 hours or overnight. Spoon on whipped cream and serve.

Makes 1 9-inch pie

PECAN TARTS

4	eggs, beaten	1/4	teaspoon salt
1 1/2	cups dark brown corn sugar	1 1/4	cups chopped pecans Unbaked pastry for 14 to 18 tart shells (page 185)
1 1/2	tablespoons melted butter		
1 1/2	teaspoons vanilla extract		

*B*eat the eggs, sugar, melted butter, vanilla extract, and salt. Add the nuts and mix lightly. Pour into pastry-lined tart pans and bake in a preheated 400° oven for 10 minutes. Reduce the heat to 300° and bake for 20 to 30 minutes, until the filling is set.

Makes 14 to 18

HONEY NUT TART

Dough

1/2	cup sugar	2 1/2	cups sifted flour
2	sticks (1 cup) butter		Pinch of salt
1	egg plus 1 egg yolk		

Filling

2/3	cup sugar	2	tablespoons honey
3	tablespoons butter	3	cups mixed nuts
2	tablespoons water		(walnuts, pecans,
1/2	cup heavy cream		sliced almonds)

*I*n an electric mixer at low speed, combine the sugar and butter. Add the egg and yolk, then the flour and salt. Knead into a ball and refrigerate for 1 hour. On a floured surface, roll out the dough to fit a 9-inch tart pan. Bake the shell in a preheated 375° oven for 10 minutes.

For the filling, cook the sugar with butter and water until dissolved. Continue cooking until the mixture caramelizes and turns a golden tan. Remove from the heat and stir; gradually add the cream. Add the honey and cook for 1 minute, making sure the lumps are out. Add the nuts and coat them well with the caramel. Pour into the tart shell and bake in a preheated 350° oven for 20 to 25 minutes. Let cool completely before serving.

Makes 1 9-inch tart

From Jo Anne Gretta, pastry chef instructor: "A favorite German recipe I found in Santa Barbara, California."

Cheesecake

*A*s these recipes show, there is much to be said about cheese-cake, and there are many ways to make it.

RICH CREAM CHEESE CAKE

Shortbread

1³/4 cups sifted flour
1 stick (8 tablespoons)
  butter, cut into
  small pieces
5 tablespoons sugar

1 egg yolk
Pinch of salt
Grated zest of 1
  lemon

Filling

1 cup milk
³/4 cup plus 2 tablespoons
  granulated sugar
Pinch of salt
Grated zest of 1 lemon
4 egg yolks

2 envelopes unflavored
  gelatin, softened in
  cold water
2 cups heavy cream
1 pound cream cheese
Powdered sugar

Sift the flour onto a clean work surface or into a large bowl. Dot with the butter. Make a well in the center and add the sugar, egg yolk, salt, and lemon zest. Working from the center outward, quickly knead all of the ingredients into a smooth dough. Press into a ball, wrap in foil or plastic wrap, and refrigerate for 2 hours.

Heat the oven to 375° and grease 2 cookie sheets. On a floured surface, roll out the dough to make 2 10-inch rounds. Place them on the cookie sheets, and pierce one of them all over with a fork, to keep it from rising unevenly during cooking. Bake for 8 to 10 minutes, until golden brown. While still warm, cut the pierced round into 16 wedges. Let cool on a rack with the other round.

To make the filling, put the milk, granulated sugar, salt, lemon zest, and egg yolks in the top of a double boiler over simmering water. Heat gently, stirring constantly, until smooth and slightly thickened. Remove the lemon custard from the heat and transfer to a mixing bowl. In a small saucepan, dissolve the gelatin in 3 tablespoons water over low heat. Stir into the lemon custard; let cool. Whip the cream until stiff. Beat the cream cheese to soften it. When the custard begins to set, stir in the cream cheese. Put the mixture in a blender and process until smooth. Return it to the bowl and carefully fold in the whipped cream.

Line the sides of a 10-inch springform pan with a strip of wax paper and place the whole shortbread round in it. Spoon in the cream cheese filling and smooth the surface. Arrange the shortbread wedges on top to form a round. Refrigerate until set. Remove the cheesecake from the pan and carefully peel away the wax paper. Sift powdered sugar on top.

Serves 16

GRAPE CHEESECAKE

Cake

4 eggs, separated	Scant 1/2 cup sifted cornstarch
3 tablespoons lukewarm water	1 teaspoon baking powder
2/3 cup sugar	
1 cup sifted flour	

Filling and Topping

1 pound cream cheese	8 ounces black grapes, halved and seeded
2 egg yolks	4 ounces seedless green grapes, halved
2/3 cup sugar	
Juice of 1 lemon	1/2 cup grape jelly
1 envelope unflavored gelatin, softened in cold water	1 cup toasted sliced almonds
1 cup heavy cream	

*B*utter the bottom and sides of a 9-inch springform pan. Heat the oven to 375°. Beat the egg yolks, water, and half of the sugar in a large bowl until pale and creamy. Beat the egg whites until stiff; fold in the remaining sugar. Fold into the egg yolk mixture. Sift together the flour, cornstarch, and baking powder. Fold into the egg mixture. Pour into the springform pan and bake for 40 minutes, or until a toothpick inserted in the center comes out clean. Let cool on a rack for 2 hours.

To make the filling, beat the cream cheese, egg yolks, sugar, and lemon juice. Dissolve the gelatin in 2 tablespoons water over low heat. Let cool slightly. Whip the cream until stiff and fold it into the cheese mixture, along with the gelatin. Cut the cake into 2 layers. Fill with half of the cream cheese mixture, top with the other layer, and spread the rest of the filling over the top and sides of the cake. Arrange the grapes on top in any design you like. Warm the jelly and drizzle it over the black grapes. Press almonds onto the sides of the cake and refrigerate to chill.

Serves 16

PEAR CHEESECAKE

Praline

3/4   cup sugar

3/4   cup coarsely chopped almonds

Pastry

1 1/4   cups sifted flour
        Pinch of salt
7   tablespoons butter,
        cut into small
        pieces

3   tablespoons sugar
    Few drops of vanilla
        extract
1/2   beaten egg

Filling

1	1-pound can pear halves, undrained		Juice of 1 lemon
1/4	cup kirsch	1	envelope unflavored gelatin, softened in cold water
9	ounces cream cheese		
1/2	cup plus 2 tablespoons sugar	1	cup heavy cream
		1/3	cup red currant jelly

*H*eat the sugar and almonds in a medium saucepan over low heat. When the sugar has dissolved, boil slowly until golden. Pour the mixture onto an oiled cookie sheet and let it set. When cooled, crush the praline with a rolling pin and set aside.

To make the pastry, sift the flour and salt into a mixing bowl. Using a pastry blender, cut in the butter evenly. Mix in the sugar, vanilla extract, and egg to make a dough. Wrap in foil or plastic wrap and refrigerate for 2 hours.

Heat the oven to 400°. On a floured surface, roll out the dough to fit an 8-inch flan pan with a removable bottom. Place the dough in the pan and pierce it at close intervals. Cover with a sheet of baking foil or regular foil and weight it with dried beans. Bake for 30 minutes or so, until golden. Let cool on a rack.

To make the filling, drain the pears and reserve 3 tablespoons of the juice. Moisten the pears with a little kirsch. Beat the cream cheese, 1/2 cup sugar, lemon juice, and remaining kirsch in a medium-size bowl. Dissolve the gelatin in the reserved pear juice over low heat. Let cool slightly and stir into the cheese mixture. Refrigerate. Whip the cream with the remaining 2 tablespoons sugar. Mix two thirds of the whipped cream with 3 tablespoons praline and half of the jelly. Spread over the cheesecake. Fill a pastry tube with a star tip with the remaining whipped cream and decorate with rosettes. Decorate with the remaining jelly, heated, and garnish with 1 tablespoon praline. Refrigerate until ready to serve.

Serves 16

FRENCH CREAM CHEESE CAKE

Crust

1	cup graham cracker crumbs	4	tablespoons sugar
4	tablespoons melted butter	1/8	teaspoon cinnamon

Filling

1	pound cream cheese	1 1/2	teaspoons vanilla extract
4	eggs, separated	1	cup sour cream
1/2	cup sugar		

*M*ix all of the crust ingredients, press into a 10-inch pie pan, and chill.

Mix the cream cheese and egg yolks and beat until well mixed and light. Add 1/4 cup sugar and 1/2 teaspoon vanilla extract. Beat again. Beat the egg whites separately until stiff. Fold into the cheese mixture and pour into the pie shell. Bake in a preheated 350° oven for 25 to 30 minutes. Let cool, then top with a mixture of the sour cream and the remaining sugar and vanilla extract. Bake at 450° for 5 minutes.

Makes 1 10-inch cake

My own, and a favorite.

JEFF BROOKS'S CHEESECAKES

3	pounds cream cheese	2	tablespoons cognac
3/4	cup plus 1 tablespoon sugar	2	9-inch graham cracker pie shells (double the preceding recipe) pressed into 2 9-inch springform pans
7	eggs		
1/3	cup cornstarch		
	Dash of lemon extract		
	Dash of vanilla extract		

*H*eat the oven to 300°. Whip the cream cheese until smooth. Add the sugar, eggs, cornstarch, extracts, and cognac. Strain it to get out all the lumps, or blend in a food processor until smooth. Pour into the pie shells. Set a pan of boiling-hot water in the bottom of the oven, and put the springform pans over it. Bake for 2 hours. Take the sides off the springform pans and let the cheesecakes cool on a rack before removing the pan bottoms.

Makes 2 9-inch cheesecakes

Variations: Top with a fruit glaze or a mixture of sour cream and sugar to taste, then cooked cut-up fruit, or just use the fruit. Also good is plain whipped cream.

CHEESECAKE IN
A REGULAR PIE CRUST

1 tablespoon flour	1/2 teaspoon vanilla
1/2 cup sugar	extract
8 ounces cream cheese	1/8 teaspoon lemon juice
2 eggs	1 8-inch pie shell (page
1/2 cup light cream	185)

*C*ombine the flour and sugar and work in the cream cheese. Beat in the eggs, one at a time. Gradually stir in the cream and add the vanilla extract and lemon juice. Partially bake the pie shell; while it is still slightly warm, pour in the mixture and cover the exposed crust with foil. Bake in a preheated 350° oven for 40 to 50 minutes. Let cool, and top with your favorite topping.

Makes 1 8-inch cheesecake

ITALIAN CHEESECAKE

1	pound cream cheese	1	teaspoon vanilla	
1	pound ricotta cheese		extract	
1¹/2	cups sugar	1¹/2	teaspoons lemon juice	
4	eggs, slightly beaten		Grated zest of 1	
3	tablespoons		lemon	
	cornstarch	1	pint sour cream	
3	tablespoons flour	8	tablespoons melted	
			butter (1 stick)	

*H*eat the oven to 325°. Mix the cream cheese and ricotta. Add the sugar and mix well. Add the eggs, then the cornstarch, flour, vanilla extract, and lemon juice and zest. Add the sour cream and melted butter and mix. Pour the batter into a buttered 9-inch springform pan and bake for 1 hour, or until the cake is set in the center. Turn off the heat and leave the cake in the oven for 2 hours more. Remove and let cool at room temperature.

Makes 1 9-inch cheesecake

TORTE DI RICOTTA

1/2	cup toasted almonds	1	9-inch partially baked
1¹/2	pounds ricotta cheese		pie shell plus pie
1	tablespoon chopped		crust for lattice top
	citron		(page 185)
4	eggs	2	tablespoons powdered
1/3	cup granulated sugar		sugar
1	teaspoon vanilla		
	extract		

*F*inely chop the almonds; add the ricotta and citron and mix thoroughly. Beat the eggs and granulated sugar well; add the vanilla extract. Add to the ricotta and stir until well blended and smooth. Pour the filling into the pie shell and place latticework strips over the top. Wet the edges and pinch them together; cover them with foil to prevent burning. Bake in a preheated 360° to 375° oven for 45 minutes, or until the mixture is firm but not dry to the touch and the pie crust is golden brown. Remove from the oven and let cool. Sprinkle with powdered sugar.

Serves 10 to 12

SOUR CREAM CHEESECAKE

2	sticks (1 cup) butter, at room temperature	1/2	teaspoon salt
		1/4	teaspoon baking soda
2 3/4	cups sugar	3/4	cup sour cream
6	eggs, at room temperature	1/2	cup cream cheese
		12	teaspoons vanilla extract
3	cups sifted flour		

*H*eat the oven to 350°. Butter and flour a 10-inch tube pan. Cream the butter and sugar, using an electric mixer. Add the eggs, one at a time, beating well after each addition. Sift the flour with the salt and baking soda, and add to the butter mixture in three batches, alternating with the sour cream and cream cheese and mixing well after each addition. Blend in the vanilla extract. Pour the batter into the pan and bake for about 1 1/4 hours, until the top is light brown and a tester inserted near the center comes out clean. Let cool in the pan.

Makes 1 10-inch cheesecake

LOW-CALORIE CHEESECAKE

1	teaspoon butter	2	teaspoons vanilla extract
2	tablespoons bread crumbs	1	tablespoon grated lemon zest
3 1/2	cups cottage cheese	4	large eggs, separated
1/2	cup sifted cornstarch		
1/2	cup plus 2 tablespoons sugar		

*H*eat the oven to 350°. Lightly butter the sides and bottom of a 9-inch springform pan. Press the bread crumbs smoothly over the bottom of pan to line it. In an electric mixer, beat the cottage cheese, cornstarch, 1/2 cup sugar, vanilla extract, lemon zest, and egg yolks until smooth. In another bowl, beat the egg whites until they peak; add the 2 tablespoons sugar, a little at a time. Fold the egg whites into the other mixture, then pour into the pan and bake for 55 minutes. Turn off the oven and leave the cake in it for another hour. Take it out and let cool on a rack. Do not chill it. Cut into quarters and serve as is or with a fruit topping made without sugar.

Makes 1 9-inch cheesecake

Cookies

Most people have cookie thieves at home, and I honestly believe many of us make cookies just to enjoy catching them. We seem to have a voracious appetite for them, too. For pure enjoyment, these recipes are at the top of the list.

CHERRY AND SESAME COOKIES

2   sticks (1 cup) butter
1/4 cup sugar
1   teaspoon almond
    extract
2   cups flour

1/4 teaspoon salt
    Sesame seeds
1/3 cup halved candied
    cherries

*I*n a mixing bowl, cream the butter and sugar until light and fluffy. Add the almond extract, flour, and salt. Beat until just mixed. Refrigerate to chill. Shape into 1-inch balls, roll in sesame seeds, press a cherry half on top, and bake on greased cookie sheets in a preheated 400° oven for about 10 minutes. Let them sit in the oven for another 2 to 3 minutes, then put them on a rack to cool.

Makes 3 dozen

HERMITS

1/2 cup shortening
2   eggs
1/2 cup plus 2
     tablespoons sugar
2/3 cup molasses
13/4 cups flour
11/2 teaspoons cinnamon

3/4 teaspoon ginger
3/4 teaspoon baking soda
1/2 teaspoon salt
1/2 cup seedless raisins
1/2 cup chopped walnuts
     or pecans

*I*n an electric mixing bowl, cream the shortening, 1 egg, and the 1/2 cup sugar. Add the molasses and beat until fluffy. In another bowl combine the dry ingredients. Add them to the creamed mixture. Fold in the raisins and nuts. Divide into 2 portions, transfer to a greased cookie sheet, and shape into 2 12 × 2-inch rectangles. Bake in a preheated 360° oven for about 15 minutes, then take them out and brush them with a glaze made from the remaining egg and sugar, beaten together. Cut into bars while still warm and let cool on a rack.

Makes 3 dozen

BANANA GRANOLA COOKIES

1/2	cup shortening	3	ripe bananas, well mashed
1	cup brown sugar	1	teaspoon cinnamon
11/2	cups flour	1/2	teaspoon salt
1	egg	1/2	teaspoon baking soda
1/2	teaspoon vanilla extract	1	cup granola

*I*n a blender, mix the shortening and sugar. Add the flour, egg, vanilla extract, and bananas. Blend well. Add the cinnamon, salt, and baking soda. Blend again. Stir in the granola. Drop onto greased cookie sheets by the teaspoonful. Bake in a preheated 360° to 375° oven for about 12 minutes. Let cool on a rack.

Makes about 48

CHOCOLATE CHIP DROP COOKIES

2	sticks (1 cup) butter, softened	2	cups plus 4 tablespoons sifted flour
1	cup brown sugar	1	teaspoon salt
1	cup granulated (white) sugar	11/2	teaspoons baking soda
2	eggs	1	cup chopped walnuts, pecans, and/or almonds
1	teaspoon vanilla extract	1	cup chocolate chips

*C*ream the butter and gradually add the sugars; heat in a saucepan until creamy. Transfer to a mixing bowl and beat in the eggs and vanilla extract. Sift together the dry ingredients and stir into the butter mixture. Stir in the nuts and chocolate and mix well. Drop by the tablespoonful onto greased cookie sheets and bake in a preheated 375° oven until slightly browned. The centers should still be soft.

Makes 24 to 30

MERINGUE CUPS

3	egg whites, at room temperature	6	ounces unsweetened chocolate, melted
1	cup sugar	1/2	teaspoon vanilla extract

*H*eat the oven to 350°. Grease 2 cookie sheets with clarified butter and set aside. In a mixing bowl, beat the egg whites to the soft-peaks stage. Add the sugar, a little at a time, and beat until stiff. Fold in the chocolate and vanilla extract. Shape the meringue into cups on the cookie sheets and bake for at least 15 minutes. Let cool on a rack.

To use, set them on dessert dishes, fill with fresh fruit, and top with a nice rich brandied cream sauce (page 260).

Makes 4 to 6

OTHER
DESSERTS

FRIED DOUGH

6 cups lukewarm milk (100°)
6 tablespoons granulated sugar
2 teaspoons salt
2 compressed yeast cakes, crumbled
4 eggs
6 tablespoons shortening
7 cups sifted flour
Fat for deep-frying
Nutmeg
Powdered sugar

*M*ix the milk, granulated sugar, and salt. Add the yeast, then stir in the eggs and shortening. Mix in the flour, using your hand to blend it well. Knead for at least 10 to 15 minutes. Set it aside, covered, to rise until doubled in bulk. Punch it down and let it rise again. Make a ball out of it, and set it aside to rest and rise a bit more, 15 minutes or so. Cut the pieces to whatever size and shape you wish and deep-fry them in 375° fat, turning them once the underside has browned to your satisfaction. When they are fully cooked, do as the Amish do—mix a bit of nutmeg with powdered sugar and sprinkle it on the hot dough as soon as it comes out of the fat. I love to eat them just as they are, but you can put anything on yours, so long as you enjoy.
    Makes 18 pieces

Many of us go for the tasty, fabulous-smelling fried dough often seen on stands at a fair or in the window of a specialty restaurant. They are all really great and I find no fault with any of them, but I can honestly say that this recipe, which I begged for in the Amish country of Pennsylvania, is something to behold.

CALAS TOUT CHAUDS

2 cups cooked rice
3 eggs, well beaten
1/2 teaspoon vanilla
  extract
1 teaspoon granulated
  sugar
1/4 teaspoon salt

6 tablespoons flour
3 teaspoons baking
  powder
Fat for deep-frying
Sifted confectioner's
  sugar

Combine the rice, eggs, and vanilla extract and mix thoroughly. Stir in the granulated sugar, salt, flour, and baking powder. Drop into hot (360°) deep fat by the spoonful and fry until golden brown. Drain on absorbent paper, sprinkle with confectioner's sugar, and serve very hot.
Makes 18 fritters

CREOLE PRALINES

3 cups sugar
1 cup light cream or
  rich milk
1 teaspoon vanilla
  extract

2 1/2 cups pecans or mixed
  pecans and black
  walnuts
Dash of salt

In a heavy skillet, cook the sugar with 2 to 3 tablespoons water until caramelized. In a large saucepan, heat the cream to a simmer. Carefully pour in the caramel and cook, stirring with a long-handled spoon, until a small amount dropped into cold water forms a soft ball (236° on a candy thermometer). Remove from the heat and let cool to lukewarm. Add the vanilla extract, nuts, and salt, and beat until stiff and creamy. Drop onto a buttered cookie sheet and let cool.
Makes about 20 3-inchers

CARAMEL BUTTERCREAM
WITH PECAN PRALINE

Praline

1¹/2 cups shelled pecans   ¹/2 cup water
1 cup sugar

Buttercream

4 sticks (1 cup) unsalted   ¹/2 cup plus 2 tablespoons
    butter, softened   water
1 cup sugar   10 egg yolks

*T*oast the nuts in a preheated 375° oven until lightly browned, about 5 to 6 minutes. In a heavy 1¹/2- to 2-quart saucepan, dissolve the sugar in the water over medium heat, stirring. Boil without stirring until the syrup turns a light caramel color, 6 to 8 minutes. Add the nuts and stir with a wooden spoon until they are completely covered with caramel and begin to make a popping sound, 2 to 3 minutes. Immediately pour onto a well-oiled heavy tray or marble surface and spread out as rapidly as possible. When hardened, about 10 minutes or so, break into pieces and grind in a food processor to make a powder. Be careful not to grind it too much or it will turn to paste.

In a large bowl, cream the butter until light and fluffy. Set aside. In a heavy 2- to 3-quart saucepan over low heat, dissolve the sugar in the ¹/2 cup water, stirring. Bring to a boil and boil without stirring until the syrup turns an amber caramel color, 6 to 8 minutes. Brush down any sugar crystals on the sides of the pan with a heavy brush dipped in cold water. Remove from the heat and let cool for 1 minute.

In the large bowl of an electric mixer, beat the egg yolks until fluffy and lemon-colored. When syrup has cooled for 1 minute, tip the pan away from you, to avoid spattering, and carefully add the remaining 2 tablespoons water. With the mixer on high speed, very slowly pour the caramel syrup down the sides of the bowl, into the egg yolks. (Be careful not to pour onto the beater, or the syrup will spatter.) Continue beating at high speed until cool, about 5 to 7 minutes. Gradually beat in the creamed butter. Add the praline and combine thoroughly. Refrigerate until thick, about 30 minutes. Serve as is or use as a pie filling.

Makes about 4 cups

Caramel is sugar cooked until it is one step short of being burned. It is both simpler and more delicate than it appears and can be mastered easily. While expert chefs can simply cook sugar in a pan or skillet until it turns to caramel—which happens in the blink of an eye—most cooks add water to the sugar to give themselves some leeway in coping with sugar's otherwise treacherous temperament. As the sugar cooks, the water evaporates and the sugar progresses through several stages: soft ball (234° to 240°), hard ball (250° to 268°), soft crack (270° to 290°), hard crack (300° to 310°), and finally caramel (320° to 338°), when it turns from clear honey to amber in color. As soon as the bubbles become large and close together, watch it very carefully or the syrup will burn.

LEMON SOUFFLÉ

3   eggs, separated
    Scant 1/2 cup
       superfine (castor)
       sugar
    Juice and finely
       grated zest of 2
       lemons

11/2   tablespoons
         unflavored gelatin,
         softened in cold
         water
1/4   pint double or heavy
         cream
      Chopped nuts

*L*ightly butter a 1-pint soufflé dish. Cut a strip of greaseproof paper, twice the height of the dish plus 3 inches, and long enough to go around it. Fold down the 3 inches, butter the strip just made, and tie the paper, buttered side in around the outside of the dish.

Put the egg yolks, sugar, and lemon juice and zest in a heatproof mixing bowl. Set the bowl over a pan of hot water and whisk until the mixture is thickened and creamy. Remove from the heat and whisk to cool it. Dissolve the gelatin in 3 tablespoons hot water and whisk into the egg mixture. Whip the cream to the soft-peaks stage and fold it in. Cool by whisking or refrigeration.

Whisk the egg whites to the stiff-peaks stage. When the cream mixture is just about to set, fold in the egg whites. Pour into the soufflé dish and refrigerate until firmly set. Carefully ease the paper away from the soufflé with the back of a knife. Decorate with chopped nuts pressed around the sides and rosettes of whipped cream on top. Serve as soon as possible.

Serves 4

Variations: Apricot Soufflé. Omit the lemon juice and zest; instead use 1/2 cup apricot purée and the juice of 1/2 lemon. Add them after cooking and cooling the egg yolks and sugar.

Strawberry Soufflé. Omit the lemon juice and zest; use 1/2 cup strawberry purée.

ORANGE SOUFFLÉ

2   envelopes unflavored
    gelatin
1   cup cold water
8   eggs, separated
2   6-ounce cans frozen
    orange juice
    concentrate,
    thawed

1   cup plus 3
    tablespoons sugar
1½   cups heavy cream,
     chilled

*S*prinkle the gelatin in the cold water and let it soften for about 5 minutes. Meanwhile, beat the egg yolks with a whisk or electric beater until they are thick and yellow. Beat in the gelatin. Cook the mixture in a small enameled or stainless-steel saucepan over moderate heat, stirring constantly, until thickened enough to lightly coat a spoon. Do not let it come to a boil or it will curdle. Take the pan off the heat and quickly stir in the orange juice concentrate. Transfer the mixture to a large bowl and refrigerate for about half an hour, until it has thickened to a syrupy consistency.

Beat the egg whites until they begin to froth, then slowly pour in 1 cup sugar and beat until the whites form stiff peaks on the beater blades. In another bowl, whip 1 cup cream until it holds its shape softly, then beat into it the remaining 3 tablespoons sugar. With a rubber spatula, gently fold the whipped cream into the orange mixture, mixing thoroughly. (If the mixture has set too firmly and formed lumps, first beat it gently with a whisk or rotary beater.) Fold in the egg whites until no streaks of white show. Tie a piece of paper around a 1½-quart soufflé dish, about 2 inches or so above the top of the dish. Pour the mixture into it and smooth the top with a rubber spatula. Refrigerate until firm, about 4 hours. Remove the paper collar and garnish the top of the soufflé with the remaining cream, whipped and forced through a pastry bag to make rosettes in any pattern you desire.

Serves 4

STRAWBERRY SOUFFLÉ

2	pints fresh strawberries	1/2	cup water
2	envelopes unflavored gelatin, softened in cold water	1	tablespoon lemon juice
		2	tablespoons kirsch
		3	egg whites
3/4	cup sugar	1	cup heavy cream

*C*ut a 6 × 30-inch strip of parchment paper or brown paper bag and brush one side with oil or melted butter. Tape the paper, oiled side in, around the top of a 1-quart soufflé dish.

Wash and hull the strawberries. Reserve a dozen, and purée the rest in a food processor or blender. Mix the gelatin with 1/2 cup sugar in a saucepan. Stir in the water and cook over low heat, stirring, until the gelatin dissolves. Pour into a bowl and mix in the strawberry purée, lemon juice, and kirsch. Refrigerate, but give it a stir frequently, until the mixture thickens slightly. This should take about half an hour and is really crucial to making the soufflé thick enough to stand up.

Beat the egg whites until frothy, add the remaining 1/4 cup sugar, and beat until stiff. Fold into the strawberry mixture. Whip the cream until stiff and fold it in. *Gently* pour the mixture into the soufflé dish. Refrigerate until firm, about 4 hours. To serve, carefully remove the paper, so as not to rip the outside of the mounded soufflé, and garnish with the reserved whole strawberries.

Serves 4

This is called a soufflé, and looks like one, but it is not cooked.

RHUBARB SOUFFLÉ

1/2	cup red currant jelly	1	envelope unflavored gelatin softened in 2 tablespoons cold water
2	tablespoons granulated sugar		
1	pound fresh or thawed frozen rhubarb, chopped		Shortening
		4	egg whites

| 1 cup heavy cream | 1 teaspoon vanilla extract |

*I*n a 2- to 3-quart saucepan, stir the jelly with 1 tablespoon sugar over moderate heat until melted. Add the rhubarb, cover, and cook for 5 minutes. Increase the heat to moderately high and cook for 5 to 10 minutes, stirring several times, until tender. Strain into a 1-quart saucepan and let drain for a few minutes. Cook the liquid over moderate heat for 4 to 6 minutes, until only 1/2 cup remains, and purée the rhubarb in a food processor. Remove the rhubarb liquid from the heat and stir in the gelatin. Let cool to room temperature and stir in the purée.

Cut a 3-inch piece of wax paper long enough to go all the way around a soufflé dish. Apply a film of solid shortening to the paper and tie it around the dish. In a medium-size bowl, beat the egg whites until soft peaks hold when the beater is lifted. Sprinkle with the remaining tablespoon of sugar and beat for a few seconds. In another bowl, beat the cream and vanilla extract until soft peaks form. Fold the whipped cream into the rhubarb and then gently but thoroughly fold in the beaten egg whites. Pour into the soufflé dish and smooth the surface. Refrigerate for at least 3 to 4 hours.

Serves 8

CHOCOLATE MOUSSE

| 4 ounces semisweet chocolate | 4 eggs, separated |
| 1 1/3 tablespoons water | Whipped cream |

*B*reak the chocolate into small pieces and put in a small heatproof bowl with the water. Set over hot water until the chocolate has melted. Stir it until smooth. Add the egg yolks, stir well, and let cool. Whisk the egg whites until stiff enough to stand in peaks, then fold into the chocolate mixture. Make sure the mousse is perfectly smooth. Pour it into dessert dishes and refrigerate until set. Decorate it with rosettes of whipped cream.

Serves 4

VENETIAN CHOCOLATE MOUSSE

4	ounces semisweet chocolate	4	eggs, separated, plus 6 egg whites (10 whites in all), at room temperature
8	tablespoons (1 stick) butter		
1	teaspoon vanilla extract	1/2	cup plus sugar
4	tablespoons Cointreau		Pinch of cream of tartar
2	tablespoons brewed strong coffee		Whipped cream

*I*n the top of a double boiler set over simmering water, melt and mix the chocolate and butter. Add the vanilla extract, Cointreau, and coffee. Scrape into a bowl and set aside. Wash and dry the double boiler and in it beat together and cook the egg yolks and 1/2 cup sugar for 6 to 8 minutes, until smooth, creamy, and thick. Set the double boiler top on a pan of crushed ice and whisk to cool quickly. In a mixing bowl, beat the egg whites, cream of tartar, and a little sugar until very stiff.

Mix the yolk mixture into the chocolate sauce, then mix in half of the egg whites; fold in the remaining half. Spoon into stemmed champagne or soufflé glasses, chill, and serve with whipped cream on top.

Serves 4

This recipe was the result of an error in the kitchen—an assistant added twice the amount of egg whites called for. It is my favorite chocolate mousse, smooth and light.

Custard and Pudding

SOFT CUSTARD

2 cups milk	Large pinch of salt
4 egg yolks, beaten	1 teaspoon maple or
1/4 cup sugar	vanilla extract

Scald the milk, then pour it into the top of a double boiler set over boiling water and mix in the egg yolks, sugar, and salt. Stir with a wooden spoon until it begins to get thick. Set it aside and let cool, then add the extract and chill.

Serves 4

BAKED CUSTARD

2 cups milk	1/2 cup sugar
2 pinches of salt	1 teaspoon vanilla
2 eggs plus 2 egg whites	extract
Large sprinkling of nutmeg	

Blend the milk, sugar, and salt. Beat the eggs and extra whites and add to the milk mixture. Add the vanilla extract and pour into custard cups or molds. Set them in a pan of hot water and bake in a preheated 325° oven for an hour or more. Test one for doneness: insert a small, thin knife blade into the custard and pull it out. If it comes out clean, the custard is done. If any custard shows on the blade, it is not.

Serves 4

Variation: Caramel Custard. Heat 1 cup sugar in a heavy pan over very low heat and add 1 tablespoon water. Stir continuously with a wooden spoon for about 10 minutes, until the sugar is completely melted. Remove it from the heat and *very slowly* (so as not to get splashed) stir in about 1/4 cup boiling-hot water. Pour enough of the syrup into each custard cup to fill the bottom and swirl it around the inside. Pour the cooled custard over this and bake. To serve, swirl the cups in hot water for a few seconds, invert onto a serving dish, and let the caramel pour over the custard.

BAVARIAN CREAM

5 eggs, beaten	2 cups heavy cream
1/2 cup sugar	1 teaspoon vanilla
2 tablespoons unflavored	extract
gelatin softened in	1 teaspoon Grand
1/4 cup cold water	Marnier

*I*n the top of a double boiler set over simmering water, heat the eggs until an instant-read thermometer registers 80° to 85°. Using a hand-held mixer at medium speed, beat for 5 to 6 minutes. Beat in half of the sugar. Take off the heat, beat in the remaining sugar, and continue to beat until the mixture forms soft peaks. Fold in the gelatin and refrigerate until chilled.

In a chilled bowl (or a bowl set over a basin of crushed ice), whip the cream to the soft-peaks stage; do not overbeat. Add the vanilla extract and Grand Marnier and beat until the cream is a little firmer. Fold it into the egg mixture and chill.
Serves 10

The amount of gelatin suggested produces a sturdy consistency for puff pastry desserts like cream slices and napoleons. If you intend to serve Bavarian cream as a pudding, use less gelatin, to make it softer.

RICE PUDDING

1 1/3 cups milk	1 teaspoon vanilla
Large pinch of salt	extract
1 tablespoon butter	2 cups cooled cooked
6 tablespoons sugar	rice
4 eggs	1/2 cup raisins
	1 teaspoon lemon juice

*B*eat together the milk, salt, butter, sugar, eggs, and vanilla extract. Mix with the rice, raisins, and lemon juice, place in a buttered casserole dish, and bake at 325° for about 45 minutes.
  Serves 6

Variation: White House Rice Pudding. F.D.R. started the tradition of serving rice pudding at the White House, and it has continued with various recipes. First off, substitute crushed pineapple for the raisins and add a bit more milk or cream. John F. Kennedy loved rice pudding with currants. Lyndon B. Johnson had to have *big* chunks of pineapple. Jimmy Carter loved crushed peanuts in his. Ronald Reagan loves jelly beans in his. (I cannot, in all honesty, say that the last is true.)

RICE PUDDING WITH MERINGUE

1/4	cup raw rice	1/8	teaspoon salt
1	cup water	7	tablespoons sugar
2	cups milk	1	teaspoon vanilla
2	eggs, separated		extract

*C*ook the rice and water in the top of a double boiler set over boiling water for about half an hour, until the rice swells and is dry. Add the milk and continue to cook for 5 minutes or so. Beat the egg yolks with the salt and 3 tablespoons sugar. Pour in a little of the hot milk, mix well, and add to the rice mixture. Cook until creamy. Beat the egg whites and remaining 4 tablespoons sugar until stiff. Add the vanilla extract to the rice mixture, pour into a buttered baking dish, and top with the meringue. Bake in a preheated 325° oven for 15 to 20 minutes to brown the meringue. Chill well before serving.
  Serves 6

COCONUT PUDDING

8 tablespoons (1
  stick) butter
2 cups sugar
6 eggs
1 cup half-and-half
2 to 2 1/2 cups grated
  coconut

1 teaspoon vanilla
  extract
  (optional)
Heavy cream or
  whipped
  cream

*C*ream the butter and sugar. Beat in the eggs, one by one, then the half-and-half. Fold in the coconut. Add the vanilla. Pour into a buttered 2-quart baking dish and place in a preheated 375° oven. Now you must watch it. When the pudding begins to brown, turn the browned part in. Repeat this three to five times, as the pudding thickens. Finally, let the pudding come to a golden brown all over and remove it from the oven. Serve hot with cream, or cold with whipped cream.
Serves 8

REAL INDIAN PUDDING

1 1/2 cups milk
2 tablespoons cornmeal
1/3 cup molasses
2 tablespoons butter
3/8 teaspoon salt
3/8 teaspoon ginger

3 1/2 tablespoons sugar
1/2 well-beaten small egg
1/4 cup raisins
2 large pinches
  cinnamon

*I*n the top of a double boiler set over boiling water, bring the milk to a boil, stir in the cornmeal, and cook for 15 minutes. Stir in the molasses and cook for 5 minutes. Remove from the heat and stir in the remaining ingredients. Pour into a well-buttered baking dish or individual dishes and bake in a preheated 300° oven for 1 1/2 to 2 hours. Use a toothpick to check for doneness. Serve hot or cold.
Serves 6
Note: If you want the pudding to have a soft center, add 3/4 cup cold milk along with the final ingredients.

CARAMEL PEARS IN PUFF PASTRY

1 quart water	1/2 pound puff pastry
2 cups sugar	(page 183), rolled
1 vanilla bean	out 1/8 inch thick
Juice of 1 lemon	1 egg, beaten with a
1 2-inch piece lemon	pinch of salt
zest	3/4 cup heavy cream
2 small firm ripe pears,	1/2 teaspoon vanilla
peeled but not	extract
cored, and rubbed	4 tablespoons almond
with lemon juice	praline (page 200)

*I*n a 2- or 3-quart saucepan, combine the water, sugar, vanilla bean, and lemon juice and zest. Stir over medium-high heat until the sugar is dissolved. Bring to a boil, reduce the heat to a simmer, and add the pears. Poach them until just tender when pierced with a skewer, 20 to 25 minutes, and let cool in the syrup. Drain the pears, strain the syrup, and reserve both.

Cut the pastry into 4 rectangles, 4 × 2½ inches each, and put them on a buttered heavy cookie sheet. Cut the remaining pastry into strips ½ inch wide by 4 inches long. Brush the edges of the rectangles with cold water and add strips lengthwise along two sides. Press slightly to seal them together. Prick the shells with a fork and refrigerate for at least 20 minutes. Brush the borders of the pastry with the beaten egg and bake on the middle rack of a preheated 375° oven until the pastry is puffed and golden, about 15 to 20 minutes.

In a 1- to 2-quart saucepan, boil the reserved syrup until it begins to caramelize and turn a rich golden color, about 15 minutes. You will have approximately 1 cup of reduced glaze. While the glaze is still warm, brush it on the bottom of the pastry to seal it.

In a large bowl, whip the cream until it is firm. Fold in the vanilla extract and 3 tablespoons praline powder and set aside. Cut the pears in half, scoop out the cores, and trim to fit the pastry, if necessary. Cut crosswise into ¼-inch-thick slices.

Press with the palm of your hand to fan them out slightly. Spread each pastry shell with about 1/4 inch praline cream and top with a fanned pear half. Brush the pears with more warm glaze and sprinkle with the remaining praline.

Serves 4

MARTIN YAN'S CHOCOLATE PEARS

2	pears	2	egg yolks
11/4	cups sugar	13/4	sticks (7/8 cup) butter
2	pinches of salt	1	teaspoon vanilla
3	tablespoons		extract
	cornstarch	8	ounces dark,
1/2	cup Chinese rice		semisweet, or sweet
	wine		chocolate
2	pints boiling water		

*P*eel and core the pears. In a saucepan, mix half the sugar with the salt, cornstarch, and half the wine. Whisk in the boiling water and poach the pears over low heat for 7 to 8 minutes. Remove them, cut in half, and set aside.

Beat the egg yolks with the remaining sugar and wine, and pour slowly into the sugar syrup. Cook for a few minutes. Remove from the heat and whisk in 11/4 sticks butter and the vanilla extract. Ladle into the bottom of 2 dessert dishes with a well. Place the pears upside down in the center of the custard.

Melt the chocolate with the remaining 4 tablespoons butter, to keep it from hardening too much. Fill the pear cores with the chocolate and refrigerate. Turn the pears right side up, set them back on the custard, and streak designs down the sides with the remaining melted chocolate.

Serves 2

POACHED PEARS WITH SABAYON

4	pears, cored and	4	jiggers brandy or
	halved		liqueur
1/2	cup sugar		

Sabayon

8	egg yolks	3/4	cup sugar
8	tablespoons Marsala	2 to 4	tablespoons brandy or liqueur
	Spongecake		Ice cream

*P*oach the pears in 2 quarts water with the sugar and brandy. Drain and let cool. Put the egg yolks, Marsala, sugar, and brandy in a mixing bowl (or the top of a large double boiler) and set over boiling water (not *in* it). Whisk until it becomes thick and mousselike. Place a slice of spongecake on each dessert plate, put a small scoop of ice cream on it, and set a pear half on that, cavity down. Top with sabayon.

Serves 4

This dessert can be served warm, just after you have cooked it, or chilled.

HAWAIIAN MELBA PEARS

4	scoops ice cream	1	tablespoon brown sugar
	Spongecake, sliced	1	tablespoon sliced toasted almonds
1	1-pound 10-ounce can pear halves (6 to 8 halves), drained		
		1 1/3	tablespoons Cointreau
2	tablespoons butter	1/3	cup dark rum

*M*ound scoops of ice cream on slices of spongecake. In a large saucepan, sauté the pear halves in butter and sugar. Add the almonds, Cointreau, and rum, and flame it. Place the pear halves over the ice cream and serve.

Serves 4

MIXED-FRUIT GELATIN SALAD

Fruit Mold

1 envelope unflavored gelatin	1 tablespoon lemon juice
2 cups cut-up soft fruit (peaches, strawberries, blueberries, etc.)	

Topping

1 cup whipped cream	2 tablespoons brandy
2 tablespoons mayonnaise	

*M*ix the gelatin in the mold according to the package directions. Add the fruit and lemon juice and refrigerate until firm; unmold onto a serving plate. Combine the whipped cream, mayonnaise, and brandy and spoon over the salad.

Serves 4

HOT FROZEN SURPRISE CAKE

1 poundcake	2 tablespoons butter
1 quart ice cream	1 cup brandy
3 cups mixed cut-up fruit	

*C*ut the poundcake into 3 slices lengthwise and fill the layers with ice cream. Put it in the freezer. Sauté the fruit in the butter and brandy. To serve, cut a slice of cake and ladle cooked fruit over it.

Serves 6

STUFFED ORANGES

4	oranges	1/3	cup shredded coconut
1/3	cup pitted dates cut into small pieces		White of 1 small egg
1/3	cup chopped pecans	1/3	cup superfine sugar

Cut a thin slice from one end of each orange so that the pulp is exposed. From the other end cut a fine sliver so the oranges will stand securely upright. Carefully scoop out all of the orange pulp, and discard the pith and seeds. Cut up the pulp and combine it with the dates, nuts, and coconut. Fill the shells with this mixture. Beat the egg white until nearly stiff, then gradually beat in the sugar. When stiff, spread a spoonful of the meringue over the top of each orange. Place in a baking pan and brown in a preheated 350° oven.
Serves 4

AMBROSIA

3	medium oranges	Ripe strawberries
2	ripe bananas, sliced	(optional)
1 1/2	cups grated coconut	Fresh pineapple
2 to 3	tablespoons sugar	slices or chunks
	Lemon juice to taste	(optional)

Peel the oranges and slice them crosswise; remove the seeds. Arrange the oranges, bananas, and coconut in layers in a deep glass bowl. Sprinkle each layer with sugar and lemon juice. End with the coconut on top. Let stand for at least 2 hours, preferably in the refrigerator. Add the strawberries and pineapple.
Serves 6

Variation: The addition of Triple Sec, Cointreau, or cognac to this old and original recipe from the Cajuns of Nova Scotia makes it something out of the ordinary.

BANANAS FORSTER

4	firm ripe bananas	2	tablespoons butter
	Banana or coconut		Triple Sec
	extract		Brandy or Cointreau
	Grated fresh coconut		

*P*eel the bananas and moisten them with a small amount of extract. Roll them in the coconut. In a large skillet, heat the butter until it just begins to pop. Sauté the bananas in the butter until they just begin to turn a very light brown. Add the Triple Sec and brandy and heat through. Serve the juices from the pan over each. If you like, flambé it: pour on a jigger of 151 rum and light it.

Serves 4

FRESH FRUIT SALAD

Dressing

4	cups sugar		Juice and zest of 4
4	eggs, well beaten		citrus fruits

1/4	watermelon	1/2	pineapple
1/2	cantaloupe		Juice of 1/2 lime and
2	bananas		1/2 lemon
1	bunch seedless grapes	2	tablespoons butter
1/4	box strawberries	4	jiggers sweet sake

*C*ombine the dressing ingredients in a saucepan and blend well. Cook over low to medium heat, stirring constantly, until the mixture comes to a boil. Boil for 1 minute. Remove from the heat, let cool, and refrigerate. Cut the fruit into large pieces, toss with the citrus juice, sauté in butter and sake, and serve in bowls with the dressing.

Serves 6 to 8

HAWAIIAN RICE SALAD

6	tablespoons heavy cream	1/4	cup chopped almonds
1/4	cup sour cream	1/4	cup grated fresh coconut
1	jigger rice wine	3	cups cooked rice
1/4	cup fresh coconut milk	16	candied cherries, chopped
3/4	cup chopped fresh pineapple		Dash or 2 of salt

*W*hip the cream, add the sour cream, whip again, add the wine and coconut milk, and set aside. Mix all of the remaining ingredients, and serve the dressing on top.

Serves 4

PORCUPINES

2	cups shelled pecans	1	firmly packed cup dark brown sugar
1	cup pitted dates	2	eggs
2	cups plus flaked coconut		

*F*inely grind the pecans and dates. Mix with the 2 cups coconut and the sugar and eggs. Shape the mixture into logs 4 inches long and 1/2 inch thick and roll them in more coconut. Put the logs on a lightly buttered cookie sheet and bake in a preheated 350° oven for 10 to 12 minutes.

Makes 36

Sherbet and Ice Cream

Sherbet is served between courses to make the meal more interesting by refreshing the taste buds. There was a time when fresh fruit was served to this end, but then came sherbet (or, as the fashionable say, sorbet).

ANY-FRUIT SHERBET

1   10-ounce package
    frozen fruit, thawed
1/2 cup sweet vermouth
    plus 2 tablespoons
    confectioner's sugar,

    or dry vermouth
    plus granulated
    sugar
1   cup heavy cream

*B*lend until frothy, pour into a container, and freeze. To serve, spoon into footed goblets.
Serves 4

ORANGE-LIME-APPLE SHERBET

1   lime, peeled and
    seeded
2   oranges, peeled and
    seeded
2   apples, peeled and
    cored

1/2 cup honey
1   cup milk
1   cup dry vermouth
1   cup each lime, orange,
    and apple juice

*P*urée all of the ingredients and freeze for at least 1 hour. Whip the mixture after it is frozen, and refreeze until ready to serve.
Serves 4

MELON SHERBET

1   melon
1   cup pineapple juice
1   cup dry vermouth

Juice of 1 lime and 1/2
    lemon
1/2 cup honey
1   kiwi fruit

*C*ut the melon in half, dig out the pulp, and whip it in a blender with the pineapple juice, vermouth, citrus juice, honey, and kiwi pulp. Blend until smooth. Fill the melon halves with it and freeze.

Serve between courses, as a palate refresher, or as a dessert, with whipped cream and pecans or walnuts over it.

Serves 4

STRAWBERRY CHAMPAGNE SHERBET

1 pint strawberries, washed and hulled	2 tablespoons melted chocolate or Hershey's liquid chocolate
1 cup champagne	
6 tablespoons confectioner's sugar	

*W*hip the strawberries, champagne, sugar, and chocolate. Freeze for at least 2 hours. Whip it again and serve in footed goblets, between the salad and main course.

Serves 4

Variation: If you find the sherbet too sweet for your taste, add a bit of fresh orange or lemon juice to it just before serving.

RASPBERRY SHERBET

1 package frozen raspberries, thawed	1/4 cup sweet vermouth
1 tablespoon frozen orange juice concentrate	1 tablespoon fresh lemon juice
	1/2 cup sugar
	1 egg white

*C*ombine everything but the egg white in a blender and mix thoroughly. Whip the egg white to the soft-peaks stage and fold into the other mixture. Freeze and serve.

Serves 4

ORANGE SHERBET

1 cup sugar
1 12-ounce can frozen
   orange juice
   concentrate
2 ounces frozen lemon
   juice

1 cup corn syrup
1/2 cup dry vermouth
   Grated zest of 1
   orange

*B*oil the sugar in about 4 cups water for 4 to 5 minutes. Add the remaining ingredients, mix, and freeze.
Serves 4

CRANBERRY-ORANGE-WINE SHERBET

1 cup whole
   cranberries
1 cup cranberry juice
1 6-ounce can frozen
   orange juice
   concentrate

Pulp and grated
   zest of 1 orange
1 cup sweet
   vermouth
   Dash of cardamom
2 to 4 tablespoons milk

*M*ix the cranberries, cranberry juice, orange juice concentrate, orange pulp and zest, vermouth, cardamom, and 2 tablespoons milk. Check the color; if it is still rather dark, add another 2 tablespoons milk. Mix in a blender, pour into a large pan, and freeze for an hour or so. Whip it in the pan and refreeze.
Serves 4

MANGO ICE CREAM

1¹/4 cups mango purée (from 2 large mangoes)	¹/2 cup honey
1 cup heavy cream	8 ounces plain yogurt
3 tablespoons lime juice	2 tablespoons amber rum

*I*n a large bowl, combine all of the ingredients and whisk until smooth. Refrigerate until very cold, 4 hours or overnight. Place in ice cream freezer and freeze according to the manufacturer's directions.

Serves 4

SAUCES

BÉCHAMEL SAUCE

4   tablespoons butter
4   tablespoons flour
1/2   teaspoon salt

1/2   teaspoon cayenne
        pepper (optional)
2   cups milk

*I*n a skillet, melt the butter. Take off the heat, add the flour, salt, and cayenne pepper, and blend well. Cook over medium heat, stirring constantly, until the roux bubbles and then 2 to 3 minutes more. In a saucepan, bring the milk nearly to a simmer. Pour it into the roux, mix well, bring to a boil, and cook, whisking constantly with a wooden spoon, for 1 to 2 minutes.
    Makes 2 cups

Variation: Chicken Velouté Sauce. Make the béchamel with chicken stock instead of milk. To vary this, add sherry to taste.

MORNAY SAUCE

3   egg yolks, slightly
        beaten
1/4   cup heavy cream
2   tablespoons melted
        butter

2   cups hot béchamel
        sauce
2   tablespoons grated
        Swiss cheese
1   tablespoon grated
        Parmesan cheese

*M*ix the egg yolks, cream, and melted butter, then blend with the béchamel and cook, over low heat or in the top of a double boiler over simmering water until the sauce reaches a simmer. Add the cheeses and mix well.
    Makes 3 cups

Variations: Use other cheeses, such as Monterey Jack and cheddar.
    Sherry Mornay Sauce. Add sherry to taste.

SUPRÊME CREAM SAUCE

1 cup chicken velouté sauce	About 1 cup heavy cream
4 egg yolks	

*E*nrich the sauce with egg yolks, add cream to the desired consistency, and mix well. Keep it warm until needed. Do not overheat it or it will break.

Makes 2 cups

CHEDDAR CHEESE SAUCE

1 pound cheddar cheese, grated	1¹/2 teaspoons Worcestershire sauce
2 teaspoons dry mustard	2 to 3 dashes Tabasco sauce
2 teaspoons paprika	Salt
¹/2 cup milk	White pepper
1³/4 quarts béchamel sauce	

*P*ut the cheese, mustard, paprika, and milk in a saucepan. Mix with a wooden spoon. Add 1 cup of the béchamel and heat until cheese is melted, stirring constantly. Add the rest of the béchamel and the Worcestershire sauce and Tabasco sauce. Bring to a boil, beating constantly with a whisk. Add salt and pepper, and strain through a chinois. Use for macaroni and cheese, on pasta, with cooked vegetables, etc.

Makes 9 cups

Unlike most cheese sauces, this can be kept on hand in the freezer.

NEWBURG SAUCE

2 tablespoons butter	3 cups béchamel sauce
1 teaspoon paprika	Salt
1 cup dry sherry	White pepper

*M*elt the butter in a saucepan and cook paprika in it for 2 to 3 minutes, blending well. Add the sherry, mix, and bring to a simmer. Add the béchamel and whip briskly to mix well. Let it simmer for 5 minutes, then season with salt and pepper. Strain it through a stainless-steel screen and use for a Newburg dish.
Makes 1 quart

There is more than one way to make a good Newburg sauce. The most common is to start with a cream sauce.

The second method is definitely unusual, but effective no end. If you want the color usually seen in a Newburg sauce, add paprika to the cream in the very beginning, or add about 1 tablespoon tomato paste with the butter.

	Lobster or shrimp shells	2	cups heavy cream
1	teaspoon finely chopped shallot	6	egg yolks
1	teaspoon dry or semisweet sherry		

*D*ry the shells in a low oven. Pulverize them, put them in a saucepan, and add the shallot and sherry. Heat the cream in the top of a double boiler, add the yolks, and stir constantly until the sauce begins to thicken. Strain the shell mixture and add the juice to the cream sauce.
Makes about 2 cups

Variation: Thermidor Sauce. Sauté mushrooms in a little butter and sherry and add it to the sauce. For lobster thermidor, put lobster meat in it, fill a lobster shell with the mixture, and bake it.

ONION CREAM SAUCE

4	tablespoons butter	1	egg, well beaten
4	tablespoons all-purpose flour	1/2	teaspoon salt
2	cups light cream	1	tablespoon minced fresh parsley
2	tablespoons minced onion		

*H*eat the butter until it foams, then stir in the flour and cook for 2 to 3 minutes. Add the cream slowly, making it as thick as a béchamel sauce, or as thick as you want it to be. Add the onion. Let it all simmer for 10 minutes, then quickly whip in the egg and salt. Add the parsley and serve it under your dinner entrée.

Makes 2 cups

HOLLANDAISE SAUCE

2	egg yolks	1	cup hot clarified butter
	Salt		Lemon juice
2	teaspoons water		Dash of cayenne pepper

*R*emove the membrane from the egg yolks and put the yolks in a stainless-steel bowl. Add a small pinch of salt and whip slightly. As soon as the yolks darken, add the water and whip to a froth, at least doubling the volume. Cook over low heat or in the top of a double boiler until consistency reaches the soft-peaks stage. Remove from the heat and begin adding the butter, slowly to start, then faster. Add lemon juice, cayenne pepper, and salt to taste.

Makes 1 1/2 cups

BLENDER HOLLANDAISE

4	egg yolks	1/8	teaspoon white
3 to 4	tablespoons lemon		pepper
	juice	2	cups melted butter
1/4	teaspoon salt		

*I*n a blender, combine the egg yolks, lemon juice, and salt and pepper. In a saucepan, heat the butter until it bubbles. Turn on the blender and gradually pour in the hot butter, blending until thick and smooth.

Makes 2 cups

BÉARNAISE SAUCE

2   fresh tarragon leaves
4   tablespoons tarragon
     wine vinegar

2   cups hollandaise sauce

Chop the tarragon and toss with the vinegar. In a skillet, bring to a boil, then turn the heat down low and cook until the liquid is evaporated. Whip into the hollandaise sauce.
Makes 2 cups

MARCHAND DE VINS BUTTER

2   shallots, minced
3/4 cup dry red wine
1   teaspoon glace de
      viande (available
      from L. J. Minor
      Corp.)

Pepper
4   teaspoons butter,
      softened
2   tablespoons minced
      fresh parsley
     Juice of 1 lemon

Put the shallots and wine in a small saucepan and cook until wine has almost evaporated. Stir in the glace de viande and pepper and swirl in the butter. Cook briefly to the desired consistency. Add the parsley and lemon juice, and serve over steak.
Makes 1 cup

PIQUANT SAUCE

4   ounces dill pickles
8   ounces onions
1   stick (8 tablespoons)
     butter
1   quart brown sauce
     (base available from
     L. J. Minor Corp.)

1/2 pint cider vinegar
2   tablespoons dry red
      wine
2   tablespoons chopped
      fresh parsley

*C*hop the pickles. Mince the onions, heat the butter in a large saucepan, and sauté the minced onion briefly; do not let it brown. Add the brown sauce, vinegar, and wine, and simmer for at least 30 minutes. Add the pickle and cook for 15 minutes more. Remove it from the heat, add the parsley, and refrigerate until needed.

Makes 2 quarts

MADEIRA SAUCE

1   cup brown sauce (base   1/2   cup Madeira
     available from L. J.
     Minor Corp.)

*B*ring the brown sauce to a boil in a large saucepan, then let it simmer until reduced to about three fourths its original volume. Add the Madeira and let it simmer for another 5 minutes. Strain through cheesecloth or a fine strainer and refrigerate until needed.

Makes about 11/2 cups

BARBECUE SAUCE

1	cup oil	1/2	cup red wine vinegar
21/2	cups finely blended onions	1	pint pineapple juice
31/2	cups finely blended celery	5	tablespoons prepared mustard
11/2	cups brown sugar	5	tablespoons Worcestershire sauce
3	teaspoons salt		
5	cups ketchup	2	pints water

*H*eat the oil and sauté the onions and celery until just done. Add the remaining ingredients and simmer for 30 minutes. Use hot or cold.

Makes 2 quarts

Freeze what you don't use now.

JOHNNY REB'S BARBECUE SAUCE

2	tablespoons butter	2	teaspoons liquid smoke (optional)
1	cup finely chopped onion	1	cup tomato sauce
1	cup diced celery	1	tablespoon brown sugar
1	teaspoon prepared mustard	1	tablespoon cider vinegar
1	tablespoon lemon juice	1	tablespoon chili powder
1/4	cup water		Pinch of ground cloves
1/2	teaspoon cayenne pepper	1/8	teaspoon pepper
1/2	teaspoon salt		

*I*n a medium saucepan, melt the butter over medium heat. Add the onion and sauté until golden brown. Stir in the remaining ingredients and heat to a boil. Reduce the heat and simmer, uncovered, stirring occasionally, for about 30 minutes.

Makes 2 cups

CHEF RENÉ'S BARBECUED PIG SAUCE

4	tablespoons butter	1/4	teaspoon pepper
2	medium onions, chopped	2	cups diced celery
2	tablespoons prepared mustard	2	tablespoons lemon juice
1/2	cup water	1	teaspoon cayenne pepper
1	teaspoon salt	4	cups bottled chili sauce
4	cups tomato sauce	2	teaspoons brown sugar
1	medium-size can tomato juice	2	teaspoons red wine vinegar
2	teaspoons cider vinegar		Pinch of ground cloves
2	tablespoons chili powder	1	cup dry white wine

*I*n a large pot, melt the butter over medium heat. Add the onions and sauté until golden brown. Mix in the remaining

ingredients and bring to a boil. Reduce the heat to a simmer and cook, uncovered, for about 30 minutes. Use it to baste the pig, especially the inside. (Keep the pig as moist as possible, but do not worry about the skin, which will become very crisp and dark, as it is usually not eaten. Test the pig for doneness at the thickest part of the meat at the shoulder area, inside. Once you see a complete release of clear juices, it is done to perfection.)
Makes 1 gallon

PROVENÇAL TOMATO SAUCE

	Olive oil	1	celery stalk, chopped
1	garlic clove, crushed		Bouquet garni (thyme,
1	quart chopped or		sage, bay leaf,
	crushed tomatoes		allspice)
1	small bay leaf		Salt
1	onion, chopped		Pepper
1	large carrot, chopped		Sugar

*H*eat oil and sauté the garlic. Add the tomatoes, bay leaf, onion, carrot, celery, and bouquet garni. Cover the pan and simmer for 30 minutes. Remove the bouquet garni and bay leaf, and season with salt, pepper, and sugar to taste. Either sieve the sauce or purée it in a blender. Serve over or under steak au poivre.
Makes about 1 quart

MARINADE FOR LAMB SHISH KEBAB

1	cup olive oil	1¼	teaspoons salt
½	cup salad oil	1	large pinch of
4	tablespoons vinegar		marjoram
2	tablespoons lemon		Thyme
	juice		Oregano
½	teaspoon chopped		
	garlic		

*M*ix together and marinate the lamb for 4 hours to overnight.
Makes about 2 cups

*Save the marinade and reuse it. It will keep, refrigerated, for six
months.*

POULETTE SAUCE D'ANN

1	quart chicken stock	2	tablespoons Chablis
1/2	onion, chopped	2	black olives
2	large mushrooms,		Salt
	thinly sliced		White pepper

*H*eat the stock and cook the onions and mushrooms in it. Reduce the stock by one fourth. Add the Chablis and olives and
season, but be careful with the salt. Boil briefly. If the sauce
seems too thin, strain it and reserve the solids; bring the sauce
to a boil and reduce it still more. Put the onion and mushroom
mixture back in, heat through, and serve with chicken.
Makes 1 quart

CHICKEN WING SAUCE

1	quart chicken stock	1	cup brown sugar
2	onions, finely minced	2	tablespoons
2	carrots, finely minced		Worcestershire sauce
2	stalks celery, finely minced	4	tablespoons red wine vinegar
4	tablespoons dark soy sauce	1	teaspoon grated fresh ginger

*H*eat the chicken stock and in it cook the minced onion, carrot, and celery. Add the remaining ingredients and let simmer
for 5 to 10 minutes. Use to marinate and cook chicken wings.
Makes 1 quart

SWEET AND SOUR SAUCE

3 cups chicken stock	Large pinch of
1 cup honey	cayenne pepper
1 cup brown sugar	4 tablespoons
1¹/₂ to 2 cups white wine	cornstarch
vinegar	4 tablespoons soy
2 garlic cloves, finely	sauce
minced	¹/₂ cup semisweet
4 tablespoons lemon	sherry
juice	12 tablespoons water
2 teaspoons glace de	
viande (available	
from L. J. Minor	
Corp.) or Bovril	

*H*eat the stock, add the honey and sugar, and stir to dissolve. Add the vinegar, garlic, lemon juice, glace de viande, and cayenne pepper. In a bowl, blend together the cornstarch, soy sauce, sherry, and water. Add this to the pot, and stir until the sauce thickens. Serve with cooked chicken.

Serves 8 to 12

Variation: Add pineapple chunks and small pieces of boiled or sautéed green pepper, and use pineapple juice instead of water.

This wonderful sauce keeps for three months in the refrigerator and comes in handy for leftovers.

ANN GODE'S VEAL SAUCE

2 tablespoons flour	8 each black and green
2 tablespoons butter	olives, coarsely
1 cup veal stock (deglaze	chopped
a veal-cooking pan)	2 hard-boiled eggs,
¹/₄ cup dry white wine	chopped
1 cup heavy cream	Salt
	Crushed peppercorns

*I*n a saucepan, cook the flour in frothing-hot butter for 2 to 3 minutes and add the stock and wine. When the mixture thickens, add the cream slowly, then the olives and eggs. Add salt and peppercorns to taste. Serve with veal.

Serves 4

CREOLE SAUCE

Oil or bacon fat

1 pound celery, cut into julienne

1¼ pounds peppers, seeded and cut into julienne

1 pound onions, cut into julienne

8 ounces mushrooms, cut into julienne

2 garlic cloves, crushed

2 tablespoons flour

1 1-pound 12-ounce can tomatoes, in chunks or crushed

1 1-pound 12-ounce can tomato purée

1 quart beef stock

1 teaspoon crushed red pepper

Scant 1 teaspoon salt

1 bay leaf

*H*eat oil or bacon fat and sauté all the vegetables, but do not let them brown. Add the flour to this and cook as for a roux. Add the tomatoes, purée, stock, and seasonings. Cook until the vegetables are done but not browned. Serve over fish.

Makes 2 quarts

Note: If you want the sauce to be hot and spicy, add a bit of Paul Prudhomme's Seafood Magic Seasoning. For dishes other than fish, use Nellie's Cajun Seasoning, from St. Paul, Minnesota—one of the best I have tried.

Make up a gallon and store in the freezer, or cut the recipe in half. Buy mild peppers or a mixture of mild and hot, as you like.

FISH SAUCE I

1 tablespoon butter	2 cups fish stock (base
1 carrot, finely chopped	available from L. J.
1 onion, finely chopped	Minor Corp.), heated
1/2 cup heavy cream	Salt
1/2 cup dry white wine	Pepper

*M*elt the butter and sauté the carrot and onion. Add the cream and wine and cook until thick. Add to the fish stock and season to taste.

Serves 6 to 8

FISH SAUCE II

1 carrot, finely minced	1/2 cup sauterne
1/2 medium onion, finely	1/2 cup heavy cream
chopped	Salt
1 tablespoon butter	Pepper
1/2 tablespoon flour	

*S*auté the carrot and onion in butter until soft but not browned. Add the flour and cook for 2 to 3 minutes. Add the sauterne and boil briefly, then the cream, salt, and pepper. Heat through, pour over the fish, and bake until the fish is cooked.

Serves 4

This makes enough for about 2 pounds of fish.

PESTO I

2 cups stemmed fresh	2 large tablespoons
basil	minced garlic
1 cup olive oil	1/4 cup pine nuts
	Salt

*P*rocess the basil leaves in a food processor fitted with the metal blade, or pound them using a mortar and pestle. Slowly add the olive oil, and process or stir until the mixture becomes pastelike. Add the garlic and blend well. Stir in the pine nuts and add salt to taste. Toss with hot or cold pasta, or serve with potatoes or hot or cold broiled fish.

Serves 4 to 8

PESTO II

1 cup fresh white bread crumbs (crusts trimmed)	1 teaspoon salt
	1 cup oil
1/4 cup dry white wine	1/2 cup grated Parmesan cheese
2 cups fresh basil	
3 garlic cloves	3 tablespoons grated Romano cheese
1/2 cup pine nuts	

*I*n a saucepan, combine the bread crumbs and wine and stir over low heat until the mixture becomes a smooth paste. Let cool. Put it in a blender with the basil, garlic, pine nuts, and salt, and mix at high speed until thick and creamy, about 1 to 2 minutes. Add the oil in a steady stream, almost drop by drop at first, and blend until smooth and well mixed. Pour into a bowl and gently stir in the two cheeses.

Makes 3 cups

If you keep this pesto in the refrigerator or freezer, you can easily give a fresh flavor to long-cooked dishes. Form it into small balls and use sparingly in, for example, minestrone.

CURRY POWDER

*C*urry powder, although long considered one of the most popular spices in the world, is from India but is not a true spice. It is made up of many—for example, turmeric, fenugreek, ginger, red and green chilies, cumin, cardamom, nutmeg, cinnamon, cloves, lemon grass, and curry leaves. In India each family makes its own, according to taste, and sautés it in clarified butter to intensify the flavors. When cooking Indian or curry dishes, if you want a *stronger* flavor, just use a bit more curry; for a *spicier* flavor, add more red pepper.

MINT SAUCE

1	cup fresh mint	1½	cups water
½	cup cider vinegar	1	12-ounce jar mint
6	tablespoons sugar		sauce

*C*hop the mint. Put the mint, vinegar, sugar, and water in a pot and bring to a boil. Let simmer for 10 to 20 minutes. Add mint sauce to thin it out, using to taste, and serve with lamb.
Serves 4

MAYONNAISE

½	teaspoon salt	1	heaping tablespoon
2	tablespoons lemon		Dijon mustard
	juice	4	egg yolks, at room
2	tablespoons vinegar		temperature
⅛	teaspoon cayenne	2	cups peanut oil, or 1
	pepper		cup peanut oil plus
⅛	teaspoon paprika		1 cup vegetable oil

*I*n a small bowl, dissolve the salt in the lemon juice and vinegar. Add the cayenne, paprika, mustard, and egg yolks. Stir until smooth. Slowly add the oil in a thin stream, almost drop by drop, stirring quickly with a wire whisk. Taste for seasoning.
Use immediately, or stir in 1 to 2 tablespoons boiling water and keep under refrigeration in a tightly covered container.
Makes 2½ cups

Variations: Blender Mayonnaise. Combine the first seven ingredients and 1/2 cup oil in the blender. Cover and run at low speed just until blended. Remove the cover and add the remaining oil in a slow, steady stream, drop by drop at first.

Dijon Sauce (for eggs, fish, beef, poultry, and shellfish). Make mayonnaise well endowed with Dijon mustard.

Gribiche Sauce (for shellfish and cold fish). Prepare mayonnaise with very finely chopped hard-boiled egg yolks (instead of raw yolks), seasoned and blended with vinegar and oil. Fold in chopped gherkins, capers, and the whites of hard-boiled eggs.

Green Sauce (for eggs, fish, shellfish, oysters, and vegetables). Make mayonnaise with chopped fines herbs (parsley, chives, tarragon), onion juice, and blanched, drained watercress and spinach, then perfume it with a touch of Pernod.

Tartar Sauce (for fried or broiled fish or shellfish and egg salads). Add prepared mustard and anchovy paste, or chopped pickle and lemon juice.

Aurora Sauce (for eggs, shellfish, vegetables, fish, and meat). Enhance mayonnaise with tomato purée.

Russian Sauce (for shellfish, oysters, clams). Add tomato purée, chili sauce, horseradish, and chopped celery.

To think of mayonnaise only as a sandwich spread or a salad dressing is to do it a supreme disservice. It is a classic and traditional sauce. During the summer, a cold dish accented by a cold mayonnaise sauce is refreshing, easy to digest, and highly palatable.

As with any sauce or dish, high-quality ingredients are a necessity. I find the traditional choice, olive oil, too strong for mayonnaise. I prefer peanut oil, and a half-and-half blend of peanut oil and corn oil is even lighter.

The choice of acid, too, is a matter of taste. It may be white or red wine vinegar, tarragon or cider vinegar, fresh lemon juice, or a half-and-half combination. Whether you use dry mustard or Dijon, white pepper, cayenne pepper, or a dash of a liquid hot condiment sauce, each ingredient will lend its distinctive personality to the sauce. Equal amounts of salt and sugar strike a tangy note.

The seasoning in a perfect mayonnaise should be harmonious and the texture tender yet thick. The extra time it takes to make mayonnaise by hand instead of in a blender is only minutes compared to seconds. Something magical happens when you try it by hand—your work, your creation, becomes a part, or perhaps an extension, of yourself, which contributes to the pleasure of making and serving it.

For perfect mayonnaise, follow these rules:

1. All ingredients must be at room temperature.

2. The fresher the eggs, the better the mayonnaise will be. Discard the chalaza (membrane attached to shell) and any gelatinous white threads from the yolks.

3. Dissolve the salt and sugar (if you're using sugar) in the acid, then mix it into the yolks with the other basic ingredients before you start incorporating the oil.

4. Incorporate the first few tablespoons of oil drop by drop, encouraging a good emulsion to form. Then add the rest of the oil in a very thin stream (still almost drop by drop), stirring or whisking constantly.

5. Remember that 2 large Grade A egg yolks can absorb 1 cup of oil, so 2 yolks per cup of oil plus 2 tablespoons vinegar and/or lemon juice is the correct ratio.

6. The smaller the quantity of mayonnaise, the smaller the bowl must be, and vice versa. Use a whisk in proportion to the size of the bowl.

7. Never use black pepper in any clear, white, or light-colored sauce.

8. A tablespoon of hot liquid briskly stirred in at the end will help stabilize the emulsion. This will thin the sauce at first, but it will thicken on standing.

9. If the mayonnaise curdles or separates, put 1 slightly beaten egg yolk in a clean bowl and, using a clean whisk, gradually beat in the curdled mayonnaise as though it were oil—drop by drop until it is smooth, then in a steady stream.

RÉMOULADE SAUCE I

1 cup mayonnaise	1 tablespoon chopped celery
1 tablespoon chopped fresh parsley	1 tablespoon prepared horseradish
2 tablespoons Dijon mustard	1/2 teaspoon salt
1 teaspoon paprika	1/4 cup salad oil
Dash of Tabasco sauce	1/2 teaspoon Worcestershire sauce
1 tablespoon vinegar	
1 tablespoon chopped onion	

*C*ombine all of the ingredients in a small bowl and mix until well blended. Refrigerate for several hours or overnight. Serve with shrimp, crab meat, etc.

Makes 1¹/₂ cups

RÉMOULADE SAUCE II

2 cups mayonnaise
1 tablespoon minced
    sour pickles
    (preferably
    French
    cornichons)
1 tablespoon grated
    onion
¹/₂ teaspoon anchovy
    paste

2 tablespoons minced
    capers
1 to 2 tablespoons Dijon
    mustard
2 teaspoons each
    minced fresh
    parsley, tarragon,
    and chervil, or 1
    teaspoon each of
    the dried herbs

*B*lend all of the ingredients and use when chilled.

Makes 2¹/₂ cups

CUCUMBER SAUCE

3 large firm cucumbers,
    peeled and cut
    lengthwise
    Juice of 1 lemon
1 tablespoon gelatin,
    softened in ¹/₄ cup
    cold water
1 tablespoon salt
    Dash of Tabasco
    sauce

1¹/₂ teaspoons
    Worcestershire
    sauce
¹/₂ cup mayonnaise (page
    255)
2 generous tablespoons
    sour cream
1 cup heavy cream
    Dill or dill seeds
    (optional)

*U*se a spoon to scrape out the cucumber seeds. Blanch the cucumbers in boiling water with lemon juice for 3 minutes.

Drain and purée in a blender or food processor until smooth. Add the gelatin to the hot cucumber purée and stir until dissolved. Pour the mixture into a bowl and season with salt, Tabasco sauce, and Worcestershire sauce. Set the bowl over ice and stir until the mixture becomes cold and begins to set, 3 to 4 minutes. Whisk in the mayonnaise. In another bowl, beat the sour cream and heavy cream until almost firm; add it to the cucumber mixture, stirring until smooth. Add dill to taste. Pour into a serving bowl and refrigerate for at least 1 hour.

Makes 1 quart

Serve this with vegetables or fish, especially salmon. If the cucumbers are not waxed, there is no need to peel them.

MALTESE SAUCE

1/2 cup port
1 tablespoon gelatin, softened in 1/4 cup cold water
1 6-ounce can frozen orange juice concentrate, thawed

1 cup heavy cream, firmly whipped
1/2 cup mayonnaise made without mustard
Grated zest of 1 orange

*I*n a small saucepan over medium heat, cook the port for 5 to 10 minutes, until it is reduced to 2 tablespoons. Add the gelatin and stir to melt. Stir in the orange juice concentrate. Pour the mixture over the whipped cream and blend. Fold in the mayonnaise. Garnish with orange zest and chill.

Makes 3 cups

Serve this sauce with avocados or carrots, or fruit such as apples and grapefruit, perhaps combined with walnuts.

BRANDIED CREAM SAUCE

1 cup double or heavy
    cream
1/4 cup plain yogurt

1/4 cup sour cream
1 tablespoon sugar
1 jigger brandy

*W*hip the double cream just until stiff and mix in the remaining ingredients (adjust the amounts to achieve the desired consistency).

Makes 1 1/2 cups

This sauce has numerous uses—for example, spread it on a dessert plate and place cut-up fresh fruit on top, or use it under puff pastry filled with cooked fruit.

Salad Dressings

*M*ost salad dressings have as basic ingredients oil, vinegar, and some type of seasoning.

FRENCH DRESSING

1 teaspoon salt
1/8 teaspoon pepper
1/2 cup tarragon vinegar
1/2 teaspoon prepared
mustard or 1/8
teaspoon dry
mustard

1 1/2 cups olive oil
1/2 tablespoon each
chopped fresh
basil, thyme,
marjoram, and
chervil

*J*ust mix.
Makes 2 cups

ITALIAN DRESSING

1 cup olive oil
1/2 cup red wine
vinegar
2 teaspoons Italian
seasoning

2 garlic cloves,
crushed
1/4 to 1/2 teaspoon crushed
black pepper

*C*ombine and mix well.
Makes 1 1/2 cups

BLUE CHEESE DRESSING

3/4 cup oil
1/2 pint sour cream
Very finely chopped
scallion stems
3 ounces blue cheese
1/4 cup white or red wine
vinegar, or more to
taste

Juice of 1/2 lemon
1/2 garlic clove, pressed or
minced
Small pinch each of
marjoram and
chopped dill

*M*ix all of the ingredients, leaving the cheese rather lumpy—the way most people like it.

Makes 2 cups

Variations: Change the cheese to Roquefort or cheddar, Swiss, etc.

You can also change the flavorings: use celery seed, savory, chives, lime juice, yogurt, salt and pepper. Use tarragon or apple cider vinegar.

SPINACH SALAD DRESSING

1/4 cup French dressing	Large garlic clove, minced
1/4 cup Italian dressing	
1/2 cup mayonnaise	White pepper
1 tablespoon white wine	2 hard-boiled eggs, chopped
1/2 teaspoon lemon juice	

*C*ombine all of the ingredients and mix well.

Makes about 1 1/2 cups

BASIL DRESSING

1/2 cup olive oil	1/2 teaspoon salt
2 1/2 tablespoons finely chopped fresh basil or 1 tablespoon crumbled dried basil	1/4 cup red wine vinegar
	2 large garlic cloves, minced
2 teaspoons sugar	1/2 teaspoon black pepper

*M*ix by hand or in a blender. Refrigerate until ready to use.

Makes about 1 cup

This also goes well with spinach salad.

RAW VEGETABLE SAUCE

1	quart mayonnaise	4	teaspoons Worcestershire sauce
2	teaspoons prepared horseradish	1/2	onion, grated
2	garlic cloves, crushed	1	tablespoon celery seed
1/2	teaspoon curry powder	2	tablespoons prepared mustard
	Dash of Tabasco sauce		Pepper

Mix together and serve as a sauce or dip.
Makes 3 pints

SHRIMP COCKTAIL SAUCE

1	large jar chili sauce	3/4	cup prepared horseradish
	Juice of 2 lemons		
1	bottle ketchup		

Mix the ingredients to your taste, bearing in mind that the horseradish can make it very strong.
Makes 1 quart

FRESH FRUIT SALAD DRESSING

1	pint heavy cream	1	tablespoon sugar
1/2	pint sour cream	1 to 2	jiggers brandy
6	shakes vanilla extract		

Whip the cream and blend in the sour cream, vanilla extract, sugar, and brandy.
Makes about 1 quart

APPENDIX

EQUIVALENTS

Volume Measures

60 drops = 1 teaspoon
3 teaspoons = 1 tablespoon
2 tablespoons = 1 fluid ounce or 1/8 cup
4 tablespoons = 1/4 cup
5 1/3 tablespoons = 1/3 cup
8 tablespoons = 1/2 cup or 4 ounces or 1 gill or 1 teacup
16 tablespoons = 1 cup or 8 ounces
3/8 cup = 1/4 cup plus 2 tablespoons
5/8 cup = 1/2 cup plus 2 tablespoons
7/8 cup = 3/4 cup plus 2 tablespoons
1 cup = 1/2 pint or 8 ounces
2 cups = 1 pint
1 quart = 2 pints
1 gallon = 4 quarts
1 peck = 2 gallons
1 bushel = 4 pecks

Miscellaneous

A few grains or a speck = less than 1/8 teaspoon
Pinch = As much as can be picked up between the tip of one
finger and the thumb. A large pinch = two fingers and the
thumb.
1 jigger = 2 ounces
1 minim = 1 drop
A dash = 10 drops
1 teaspoon = 6 dashes

Weight or Avoirdupois Equivalents

1 ounce = 16 drams
1 pound = 16 ounces
1 kilo = 2.2 pounds

FLOUR

For 1 cup sifted all-purpose flour, you can use any of the following (sifted):

1 cup cake flour plus 2 tablespoons all-purpose flour
1/3 cup cornmeal plus 2/3 cup flour
1/2 cup cornmeal plus 1/2 cup flour
1/2 cup bran plus 1/2 cup flour
3/4 cup bran plus 1/4 cup flour
1/2 cup rye flour plus 1/2 cup flour
1/2 cup whole-wheat flour plus 1/2 cup flour
3/4 cup whole-wheat flour plus 1/4 cup flour

SUGAR

For 1 cup granulated sugar, you can use:

1 cup brown sugar, well packed
3/4 cup honey and reduce the liquid by 3 tablespoons
2 cups corn syrup and reduce the liquid by 1/2 cup
1 1/2 cups maple syrup and reduce the liquid by 1/2 cup
1 1/2 cups molasses and reduce the liquid by 6 tablespoons

A COMPARISON OF THICKENING AGENTS

Thickener	Appearance	Amount	Use	Technique
Flour	Opaque	1 tablespoon per cup of liquid	Thin gravy, soup, or sauce.	Flour may be blended with fat in a roux or beurre manié or blended with liquid in a slurry or paste. Heat to 194° or above for maximum thickness and cook for several minutes to avoid a raw taste. Heating with acids causes thinning, and high sugar content reduces thickening power.
		2 tablespoons per cup of liquid	Medium gravy, soup, or sauce.	
		3 tablespoons per cup of liquid	Thick gravy, soup, or sauce.	
Browned flour	Opaque	2 tablespoons in place of 1 tablespoon white flour	Same as above; darker color, more flavor.	Same as above.
Cornstarch	Transparent	1 tablespoon in place of 2 tablespoons white flour	Sauces, fruit glazes, Chinese cooking.	Same as flour, but do not boil more than 3 minutes. Boil 1 minute to coagulate. Add acid or sugar only after coagulation.
Arrowroot	Transparent, sparkling	Variable; usually 1 tablespoon in place of 2 tablespoons white flour	Fruit sauces, delicate sauces, soups, gravies.	Attains maximum thickening at 158° to 176°. High sustained heat and stirring will cause thinning.
Potato starch	Translucent	1 tablespoon in place of 2 to 2½ tablespoons white flour	Gravies, savory sauces.	Same as arrowroot.
Eggs	Opaque	2 eggs will thicken 1 cup liquid	Custards, soups, sauces.	Blend with sugar or cream first, add hot liquid to egg mixture to heat slowly and raise coagulation point, then incorporate into sauce or soup. Do not boil unless sauce includes flour.

INDEX

The information in parentheses reflects the origin or the originator of the recipe.